THE
PATHOLOGICAL
GRIEVING
OF
AMERICA

OVERCOMING GRIEF ON A PERSONAL, CORPORATE, AND NATIONAL SCALE

WADE JENSEN, M.DIV.

THE PATHOLOGICAL GRIEVING OF AMERICA

OVERCOMING GRIEF ON A PERSONAL, CORPORATE, AND NATIONAL SCALE

Printed in the United States of America.

Print Version ISBN: 978-0-9960703-1-7

Electronic Version ISBN: 978-0-996703-2-4

Kindle ISBN: 978-0-9960703-0-0

Library of Congress Control Number: 2014905882

Scripture references appear in the endnotes:

To Contact the author:

www.americaschaplain.com

WHAT OTHERS ARE SAYING

"Wade's extensive experience in crisis and care ministry both in military and civilian settings serves him well towards writing about grief and how we process grief and what we need to do to not get stuck and when we do, how to get unstuck. I recommend this book because of the man of integrity and passion I've known Wade to be in the eight years I've known him."

—W. DEAN DYK, M. DIV.
CPE Supervisor and Director of Pastoral Care & Education
Swedish Medical Center, Englewood, CO

"Insightful, moving and inspirational, a must read for those who have a need to move forward in life. Sitting still and grieving takes our lives from us, and that is not God's plan, this book provides the answer to the question of why we should live for the memories of those who go before us."

—R. ALAN KING
Author of *Twice Armed: A Soldier's Battle
for Hearts and Minds in Iraq*
Winner, 2008 William E. Colby Award.

"This book is well written and interesting. I appreciate the effort and intent."

—DR. JOHN M. R. COVEY
Director, Marriage/Home/Family Initiatives
Franklin Covey

WHAT OTHERS ARE SAYING

"Chaplain Wade A. Jensen, Major, United States Air Force, offers an excellent portrayal of grief and grieving as it relates to tragedy—whether created by war, terrorism or natural disaster.

As human beings, we are all subjected to life's circumstances which can sooner or later result in confronting grief. Wade presents a realistic and objective understanding of the topic in his eloquent writing."

—TONY & JANET SEAHORN
Authors of *Tears of a Warrior*

"In a personal and engaging manner, Wade Jensen helps explain the American malaise and charts its cure by drawing on the truth and power of The Bible. The reader is sure to be challenged to look within himself, to think hard about what matters most, and to consider the claims of the living God of the Bible."

—DOUGLAS GROOTHUIS, PH.D.
Professor of Philosophy at Denver Seminary
Author of eleven books, including *Christian Apologetics*

"I have the privilege of knowing Wade Jensen. He is an expert in a rare field who will be sought out by multitudes once this book is released. Open the cover and see why!"

—DR. LANCE WALLNAU
President, The Lance Learning Group
www.lancewallnau.com

TABLE OF CONTENTS

ACKNOWLEDGEMENTS

My inspiration and motivation for this work came through several venues, and I would like to acknowledge and thank them. First, the patients and staff I have worked with at the Colorado Neurological Institute (CNI) have given me my greatest inspiration for this book. In particular, the brain tumor patients have proven time and again that even though grief and loss are powerful forces, anything can be overcome with a vision and sense of purpose. Thank you Lyn Densem-Chambers for your personal time and insight as a patient and author. Thank you Terri Spitzer for allowing me to interview you about your firsthand account of the terrorist attack in New York on September 11, 2001 and for the pictures you gave me from your camera taken on that terrible day. I present your photos in this book, untouched. Thanks also to you Dr. Edward B. Arenson, Jr. (Dr. A.), for allowing me to serve with you and interact with some of the most remarkable people on the planet.

Second, the people I have served with in the military continually display the meaning of living and serving with honor, even when politicians or the public have an ulterior motive or different opinion, respectively. The military community continues to set their face like a flint (Isaiah 50:7) and serve in the midst of adverse circumstances in uncertain times.

Third, I would like to thank Mr. Bill O'Reilly for writing his book, *Culture Warrior*, and for sharing it with those deployed in the Middle East, known to us as the "AOR" (Area of

Responsibility).[1] Some comments in his book sparked some ideas for mine.

Fourth, I would like to thank David Morrell for taking the time to visit with me and encouraging me to write a book. He came on a USO "Author Tour" in Iraq and took the time to visit with me personally and said, "I can see that you have a best seller in you and you need to write it." Thank you for sending me a copy of your "how to write book"[2] that was like giving me the boat with the oars! The time and timing of our meeting was ordained to be the push I needed to get this message from my heart to the paper.

Fifth, I would like to thank the OAK Initiative for hosting a writing seminar that I received the "Cliff Notes" from—thanks to my wife, Heather, attending while I was deployed in Iraq. This led to us attending a seminar with Dr. Lance Wallnau that dramatically impacted us and led to the right publisher for me, Wendy K. Walters.

Sixth, I would like to personally express my gratitude to Wendy. Thank you for taking the time to visit with my wife on a personal level while she was dealing with a husband who had come out of Iraq a different man from when he was deployed. Wendy, without your insight, assignments, and coaching, this would not have come to fruition in the way that it has.

Seventh, I would like to thank my parents, Jack and Diana, for being authentic people, for being willing to change, and for the perseverance that has been passed on to all six of us children. I would like to thank my dad for the inspiration as well as personal accounts of 1959. These made for a great case study for the "American Dream."

Finally, I want to thank the most important person in my life on this planet, my wife, Heather. You helped make a way for me to get this work accomplished and would push me to just "write the thing" and get it out there for people. Without your support, I could have been "throwing bags" rather than making this happen, and you above all people, know what I mean. I am eternally grateful that God saved His best wine for last.

Endnotes

1. Bill O'Reilly, *Culture Warrior*, (New York: Broadway Books, 2006).
2. David Morell, *The Successful Novelist*, (Naperville, IL: Sourcebooks, Inc., 2008).

IF ONE DREAM
SHOULD FALL AND
BREAK INTO A
THOUSAND PIECES,
NEVER BE AFRAID TO
PICK ONE OF THOSE
PIECES UP AND
BEGIN AGAIN.

—FLAVIA WEEDN

PREFACE

When I read, I call the preface the "So What?" part of the book. Much has been said and much has been written since that fateful September day in 2001, but not much has given the answers, provided the direction, or supplied the hope we need as a nation. Nothing I have encountered has been offered from the perspective I am bringing forth in the pages of this book. This is not a book of platitudes or an attempt at giving the "right" answers. I present questions from my perspective that may direct us on a path toward acceptance— and acceptance is what our nation must achieve in order to reach healing and recovery.

I am building on some very solid work by respected people in the field. The seminal work on grief and loss, *On Death and Dying*, by Dr. Elisabeth Kubler-Ross, is very well-known among those of us who work with cancer patients.[1] In addition, the follow up work with David Kessler, *On Grief and Grieving*, presents the grief cycle as the progression we all go through anytime we experience loss in our lives.[2] If you are seeing this for the first time, the stages of grief are denial, anger, bargaining, depression and acceptance, respectively.[3] Within our Western mindset, however, we might place numbers in front of each one of these stages and think, "OK, I have done number one, now it is on to step two." Then we would just continue through the countdown until we reach the end.

LINEAR ASSUMPTION

That isn't how it works. Grief is more *Confucian* in nature, which simply means that we may cycle through all the stages several times, or perhaps cycle through two or three stages simultaneously for several months (see illustration below). Grief is not just a "one time through" and we are finished. We will examine this together, and hopefully, ask the right questions to move us all the way through the process and into healing.

CYCLICAL GRIEF PROCESS

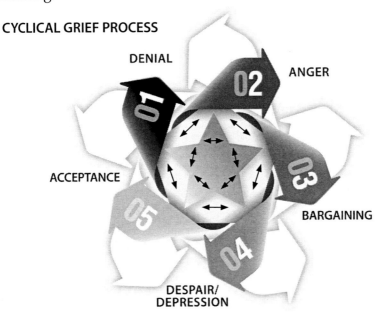

The major difference in my perspective is the power of grief having an impact, not just on an individual level, but on a community, corporate, and national level as well. I have been putting the pieces together over a three year period, and during this critical time, a mosque is proposed to be built on a site close to where the Twin Towers stood in Manhattan, known to all of us as "Ground Zero."[4] If we needed a circumstance to prove that healing still needs to take place, this is it! If our nation was a man shot in the abdomen, this would be like him saying, "I am fine," while he still bleeds. Then someone comes up and pours salt in the open wound. I assure you that the man would be screaming out in agony, letting you know that his wound is not healed—it still hurts.

Since some people do judge a book by its cover and title, I want to define what pathological grief is. Simply stated, this is when a loss happens and a person (family, community, or nation) does not come to a place of acceptance where life can continue. Rather, their life is "stuck" in that moment, and it consumes their thoughts and behavior, many times without them (the person, group, or nation affected) realizing just how trapped they are. If life is "stuck" in that time frame, then ultimately even though time keeps ticking, their life is not being lived to the fullest.

As for me, I come from rural country—Wyoming and the Dakotas—so I know what "Apple Pie America" was really like. The dimples help out somewhat too! I believe in America. I have lived in the heartland and her blood runs through my veins. As you read, I want you to consider one other aspect of me, my profession. As a chaplain, I deal with grief and loss almost daily. I have come to recognize certain patterns we all go through, regardless of race, religion, or gender. On this basis, I challenge you to dig further with me and discover just how deeply we have been impacted by the events of 9/11 and beyond.

Endnotes

1. Elisabeth Kubler-Ross, *On Death and Dying,* First Classic Scribner Edition (New York: Scribner, 1969, 1997).

2. Elisabeth Kubler-Ross and David Kessler, *On Grief and Grieving: Finding the Meaning of Grief through the Five Stages of Loss* (New York: Scribner, 2005).

3. Kubler-Ross and Kessler, *On Grief and Grieving,* p. 7.

4. Glenn Beck, "The Cordoba Mosque Proposal at Ground Zero," *The Glenn Beck Show,* Fox News, August 11, 2010.

FOREWORD

BY

DR. TOM BARRETT

Grief impacts all cultures, communities, cities, and citizens. Grief does not discriminate in relation to gender, age, or faith. Chaplain Wade Jensen demonstrates the truth of this with real life examples ranging from the personal to the national level. Everyone experiences grief at some point in their life, but not all of us process our grief in a way that allows us to come through on the other side with a functioning life, and with a positive worldview.

I have experienced my own personal losses and can reflect on how I walked through it. Just a year ago I almost got to go to Heaven. I was not afraid to walk through that door, but I grieved for what my wife and daughter would go through. Because of the prayers of my wife and my brothers and sisters in the Lord, thankfully, I am here to tell you about it. But I can also tell you that the wave of thoughts and emotions when the doctor tells you that you have minutes to live can be intolerable, and there were times when I needed more help than I was willing to ask for.

I have served as a pastor and a chaplain, assisting people in the midst of extreme loss. What do you do or say when a loved one is pulled from the bottom of a reservoir or from under the debris of a collapsed building? With the flood of grief and emotions, this is not the time to discuss the finer points of theology. Many times, the best thing to say is nothing and to simply be with the people experiencing the loss. Based on decades of experience, I can tell you I wished I had hundreds of Wade's books to give to people who were grieving.

I also host a weekly webinar and publish weekly periodicals dealing with national issues. So I was interested to see how Wade pinpoints some times in our national recent history that have affected all of our lives, both during the events and still today. I can see how much grief and loss on a national basis is filtering our words, responses, actions and reactions. This book is a "must read" for anyone who wants to deal with the heart of the matter rather than just the symptoms.

Wade has captured a broad concept and has broken grief down into practical steps with compassion and vulnerability. Americans want "fast food" answers to all of our life situations. We want to go through the drive-through and order three easy steps to deal with our grief so that we can "get on with life." But grief doesn't come with easy answers.

This book grasps the cyclical nature of grief, a foreign concept to most of us. Wade speaks on this issue with a clear authority stemming from personal loss as well as professional experiences both as a Military Chaplain and as a minister in the civilian side of life. As he likes to ask, "Do you know what replaces ten years of experience? Nothing!" Glean from his writing and apply this to your own losses, whether personal, corporate or even national.

Wade has spent hundreds of hours studying, writing and praying over this book. Consider these ways of using this great resource. If you are a leader, use in your study group or home fellowship. If you are a pastor, teach a series of sermons from it. If you are a chaplain, use these principles in your ministry. And if you are an individual who knows someone who is grieving, read the book yourself so that you can help them with your love, and give them a copy.

Wade helps us understand that grief is not an end, but rather a beginning of what God is going to do next in our lives. We can't see the joy that will come again, but God does. And He rejoices over us with singing!

—DR. TOM BARRETT

CEO, Golden Art, LLC.

GRIEF IS NOT AN
END, BUT RATHER A
BEGINNING OF WHAT
GOD IS GOING TO
DO NEXT IN OUR
LIVES. WE CAN'T SEE
THE JOY THAT WILL
COME AGAIN, BUT
GOD DOES. AND HE
REJOICES OVER US
WITH SINGING!

—DR. TOM BARRETT

CHAPTER 1

STUCK IN THE MUD

Do you know what it is like to be stuck in mud and you are not going anywhere—only deeper into the mud hole? Where I come from, we have this wonderful addition to the soil called sodium bentonite, which we simply call mud (or clay). The unique properties of this bentonite allow it to swell up and retain water, simultaneously making the new composition slicker than wet snot on a brass door knob. Suffice it to say, if you are in a ditch or caught in one of these mud holes, even if you have more torque than a 350 horsepower V8 engine and four wheel drive, you will not get out of this situation alone. Your best hope is that someone will come along with a beefed up 4 X 4 who happens to be on solid ground and that they will be close to you ... but not *too* close, and are willing to help!

Pathological grief is like that mud hole. It is not just a five step process and you are finished grieving. Grief is cyclical (see diagram on page xii) and can be like a vortex that will not let you out. The only way out of this mess must be by receiving some kind of assistance. Let me explain this on a personal level, then take it out all the way to the national level.

MY PERSONAL DITCH

I could say that my own ditch was dug for me before I was born. I love my mom and dad, but they are normal people with issues that had not been dealt with in certain areas of their life that had an adverse effect on me. My dad was a high-functioning alcoholic. According to his account, he had been like this from the moment he took a sip in high school. Due to the alcoholism, my dad could not express his love or care for me in a healthy way. I felt that my dad did not even want to spend time with me. Later, I would even blame myself for his drinking. This led to a deep ditch called rejection, and the more I tried to break free from it, the deeper I was pulled in. This rejection and loss in my childhood was like a tar-covered teddy bear that I kept hitting to get it away from me, but it clung to me even more.

For years, I dealt with these feelings, but I kept cycling back through anger—anger at my Dad, anger at God, anger at myself. Then I would go into bargaining. What if my Dad never took a drink? What if God would have set him free earlier, before I was even born? What if I would have responded in a different way and not taken it so personally? Are you getting the picture here? Does this seem familiar to you and your life story? Do you face depression that keeps sucking you in deeper and deeper? The more you try to wish it away, drink it away, or use some other form of escape, a tentacle reaches out and pulls you right back in. That was my personal journey until someone came to the rescue and was willing to help. Are you ready and willing to accept the help that you need? Or are you still practicing insanity (as Albert Einstein defines it)—doing the same thing over and over but expecting a different result?

I know many people reading this can relate to having an absent father. Perhaps he didn't abandon the family, but I have met many people who had dads that neglected them even while they lived in the same house. Some of us may have bigger "father wounds" than others, but no heart knows its own bitterness, and no one can truly share its joy.[1]

I hope that as I express the loss I felt, you will be able to relate with your own losses in one way or the other. This mud pit kept me stuck for twenty-seven years! I finally went through grief counseling in 2004, felt solid ground under my feet, and found a path out. Perhaps your personal pit has been occupied even longer than that. Now is the acceptable time to call it what it is and quit wallowing in the mire. Think of this as a popular song—country in style and being played backwards.

LITTLE DITTY ABOUT JACK AND DIANA

Jack had been a JC Penney manager at the time when Mr. and Mrs. Gowdy walked into our house. I was eight years old. My two other brothers (seven and five) were also present when they found my dad passed out on the couch from drinking too much. They took care of us boys along with my dad, put us to bed, and called my mom at work to inform her that they would keep an eye on us until she came home. My mom, Diana, was an LPN working night shifts at the local nursing home.

Up until this point in Jack's life, he was "stuck in the mud" and could not get out of it. Also unknown to him, Diana had been stashing some cash away preparing to leave him. She could not take his drinking habit anymore and did not want her sons to be raised in that kind of environment. In another three months, she would have had enough to leave Jack and start her life over without him. During this time, my brother, Mike, had been taken to a child psychologist because of his erratic behavior. Jack came to a realization of the truth that alcoholism was a problem that he could not overcome alone.

Mr. Gowdy became the proverbial "truck" that assisted my dad in getting out of the "ditch" called alcoholism. Mr. Gowdy became my dad's sponsor through Alcoholics Anonymous. He was willing to see him become free and in turn, set a family free from alcoholism's horrible repercussions.

Sometimes, it actually takes more than one truck to get somebody else out of the ditch. Jack was given leave to go through an inpatient rehabilitation program at Heartview in Mandan, North Dakota. As one of their managers, the JC Penney Company became the other "truck," not only giving him leave, but also allowing him to come back to his position. If this had not happened, perhaps Jack would have swerved right back into the same ditch. It may take more than one vehicle to help you break free. Can you identify more than one person, group, business, ministry or non-profit organization that would be able and willing to assist you? It is alright to ask for help. Asking for help is the brave thing to do.

LEHMAN WHO?

Since the turn of the century, we have had plenty of examples of corporations that have taken on business practices or made bad decisions that were not just a swerve into the ditch, but a major rollover that resulted in the whole vehicle being abandoned, beyond repair. We have seen a number of corporations crumble within the last ten years, but I want to focus on Lehman Brothers since it existed for 158 years. How could a corporation that existed for that long come to the point of collapse?

I remember that day, September 15, 2008. The question I asked was, "Lehman, who?" Up until then, I had not heard of the corporation, but I saw my personal retirement accounts lose about 47% of their value in one day. Then I suddenly cared who Lehman Brothers Corporation was, and I was not alone in suffering loss that day, mine was just in value on paper. Others lost their jobs, friends, communities and landmarks. Mr. Robinson captured that moment well when Mr. McDonald shared his personal ditch:

"I suppose in a sense, I had seen only its demise, the four-year death rattle of twenty-first century finance, which ended on September 15, 2008. Yet, in my mind, I remember the great days. And as I come to a halt outside the building, I know too that the next few moments will be engulfed by sadness. But I always stop…

Swamped by nostalgia, edged as we all are by a lingering anger, and still plagued by unanswerable questions, I stand and stare upward, sorrowful beyond reason, and trapped by the twin words of those possessed of flawless hindsight: *if only.*"[2]

I STAND TRAPPED BY THE TWIN WORDS: IF ONLY

Can you feel his unresolved heartache and loss? "… *engulfed by sadness, but I always stop … lingering anger … if only.*" This is pathological grief. Do you relate to his testimony? Perhaps something similar happened to you in your business or corporation.

Pathological grief is not reserved for the loss of a loved one or personal possession, it can be experienced on a corporate scale. This business had a member of the Lehman family at the helm from its inception in 1850 until the year 1969.[3] That is 119 years! This company ran with the same heartbeat, had the same bloodline in its fabric, weaving its way through people, departments, decisions and time. But what happened in 1969? There was no one to take the baton and run with it … and the people within the corporation knew it. They *knew* it!

Lehman Brothers was just one corporation taking its fateful, last, "Titanic" cruise. We have not even scratched the surface of the myriads of businesses, corporations, non-profits, and churches that did not go down in a "blaze of glory," but instead left scores of people, families, and communities in a state of shock and complete loss. Some organizations out there must be able to discern the need for getting out of the mud hole or steering clear from it. Do you happen to be a part of one? Are you the one that recognizes the business is in trouble and needs someone to come to their aid?

"ROCK YOU LIKE A HURRICANE"[4]

Sometimes, just being in the wrong place at the wrong time can lead to catastrophe. When I woke up on August 26, 2005, I did not picture devastation occurring on a level where the southern Gulf Coast of the United States would be crippled. When I saw Hurricane Katrina take up the entire Gulf of Mexico on the Weather Channel, my only thought was to pray, because I did not know how people were going to get through if they decided to stay. Seeing the photo imagery of a Category 5 hurricane made me cry for mercy, and I lived in Denver, Colorado then.

It didn't end with Katrina, we received the news of Hurricane Rita coming right behind her, another Category 5 storm, not only in the same season, but less than three weeks after Katrina had just slammed into the coast. Going against the odds even more, Rita made landfall within close proximity of where the eye of Katrina hit, just to the east of New Orleans at Biloxi, Mississippi. Unthinkable damage was in their wakes, leaving physical, emotional, spiritual, and psychological trauma. The scars these storms created were definitely beyond what the eye could perceive.

Shortly after these storms, the ripple effects moved beyond the region, rocking the nation as well. In Denver, we saw gas shoot up to $2.57/gallon. How many of you would gladly go back to only paying this price? People from the Gulf Coast experienced their own diaspora, being scattered throughout practically all of the other states within the Union. The loss and the trauma being too overwhelming, many have never returned to their homeland. They became sojourners who decided to place their roots in their newfound state. The opportunity to take advantage of the new home allowed for a new beginning, a new hope.

The despair of those who stayed spiraled into a sinkhole that did not have an end, it seemed bottomless. The media captured the grief process, but they did not call it that, just an emotive story. I watched denial turn to disbelief, anger turn to rage, bargaining turn to blame-shifting (what I will refer to as B.S.), and depression turn to deep despair.

We will examine reactions and realities later, but understand the process of dealing with grief and loss can affect an entire region. This is but one example that received more attention than most.

PERSONAL REGIONAL CONTEXT

There are many disasters which give us a warning of their arrival. Some are natural and some are not. Some are much more unpredictable. Some seem to have a life of their own as if they had a kind of will or passion behind their strike.

Residents of Moore, Oklahoma saw an EF5 tornado that made the nation gasp. Then tornados struck again in 2013, twice within days of each other! When there are repeated incidents, trauma or loss does not simply add to the situation. When it comes to processing grief this becomes exponential, where we may be feeling the ramifications at ten times, perhaps even one hundred times the intensity of the one event.

Since I was raised in the Dakotas, I think about Elgin, North Dakota or Spencer, South Dakota. In this part of the country, tornados and hail occur repeatedly. July 5, 1997, in Belle Fourche we had 3.5 inch diameter hail … for twenty minutes! You should have seen what my brother's car looked like, along with every other car, roof, exposed window or garden! In California there are earthquakes and wildfires. In Florida a dip in the thermometer can wipe out a whole citrus crop overnight and raise prices for the whole nation. Different regions experience different losses, perhaps numerous losses. I want you to define what they are for where you live. It might not be an "Act of God" or natural disaster, it could be something like a military base closing, or a main industry suffering like the automobile or steel industry. Consider all types of experiences that lead to shared loss in your region.

9/11

Who does not remember where they were on September 11, 2001? All who were living and self-aware remember what was on TV, what clothes we had on, and where we were when the news interrupted everything. We might even remember what we did or did not eat for breakfast that fateful Tuesday morning. Does anyone remember what life was like before that day?

Without a doubt, this single event has affected the entire United States more than any other in my lifetime, and it didn't stop at our border, it touched the world, transforming what we knew as our "normal" lives. If you do not believe me, just think of air travel. I was able to show up at the airport 30 - 45 minutes prior to my departure and have no problem getting on the plane, and my plane ride included a meal, charged no bag fees, and there was a relaxed feeling knowing that flying was the safest mode of travel. All of this has changed. Now we drive. Once the price is figured out along with the amount of time to find parking, go through security, then hope your flight is not cancelled or delayed, a seven hour drive with three children just became easier to deal with.

I do not believe a single event shifted our nation like this since Pearl Harbor. Whereas Pearl Harbor "awakened a sleeping giant," what we know of as "9/11" knocked our nation off its path into a pit, and my hope is that it does not become our Achilles' heel. The only way for this to be avoided is to get the nation shifted out of the pit and back onto the path, but this will take effort and time. Individually, we all must deal with our own grief, because we are personally the greatest agents for change. Once we have been willing to change, we can move on to the family, community, region and finally, the nation.

WE ARE PERSONALLY THE GREATEST AGENTS FOR CHANGE

Do you think that our nation is "stuck in the mud?" If so, read on. If your answer was no and you think we are just fine, please examine a few stories with me.

The first article that triggered something in me to address pathological grief was an article in the *Denver Post* on the 9/11 anniversary in 2007, "Teachers to Broach 9/11 Carefully, If at All."[5] Due to a lack of evidence, there was a lack of closure. Different teachers had different ideas about how to approach the subject of 9/11, but there was no clarity or guidance, and some just wanted to avoid it altogether. The date had become a heated political theme rather than a historical one (like December 7, 1941). By not addressing or acknowledging an event, we can go into denial, the primary step in the grieving process, but never get out due to the obscurity. This was six years after the event and the difference of opinions illustrates the lack of truth about that day. Without clear facts, this can become pathological since we may keep on denying truth, which is why we will delve into truth being so critical.

Three years later in 2010, I was serving at Joint Base Balad, Iraq, so I was a bit more sensitive to the 9/11 anniversary and was part of a ceremony with the firefighters there. *The Wall Street Journal* ran an article entitled "A More Divided 9/11 Anniversary."[6] The news of a mosque being built close to Ground Zero came out and it touched something deep in the heart of New Yorkers, and in many around the country. Obviously, the pain of that eventful day was still tangible, and to these people, it was like taking salt and rubbing it in an open wound.

Another article came out on October 28, 2010, concerning the same mosque near Ground Zero.[7] Prince Alwaleed bin Talal "urged the backers of the proposed Islamic Center not to agitate the wound."[8] He went on to state, "The wound is still there. Just because the wound is healing you can't say, 'Let's just go back to where we were pre-9/11.'"[9] Someone outside of your group can possess greater insight than anyone on the inside. In this case, Prince Alwaleed noticed something that many Americans probably have not.

OUR RESPONSE

In summary, how would any of these events be different if our response would have been different? You can ask this personally, for your family, your community, your business, your church, your city, your region, and ultimately, your nation. There is a formula that goes like this:

Event + Response = Outcome[10]

We cannot change the event because the past has gone by. We have already responded to the event and now we are living the outcome. However, what if we chose to respond in another manner? As an example, the airport security around the world magnified after this one day. Now all countries have some form of security that requires additional time, people, and resources. What if we educated people to be more vigilant as well as equipped to handle an abandoned bag, or recognize aggressive, threatening behavior? I am not talking about profiling, but I am certain my five-year-old girl is not the threat. How would this change the outcome? Maybe travel would become enjoyable again, simultaneously increasing the economy and creating more jobs. In processing grief, this is what we typically call "creating our new normal." We will examine responses along with some other aspects carefully so that in the journey, we can reach a place of acceptance along with a new hope and future that is waiting for us.[10]

POINTS TO PONDER

1. What is your personal ditch? Your family ditch? Your community ditch? Your corporate ditch? Your regional ditch?

2. Who or what can you identify as an assistant to help you get out of the mud?

3. Do you remember what life was like before the trauma that created the ditch?

4. How could a different response to the situation change the outcome?

Endnotes

1. Proverbs 14:10, NKJV.

2. McDonald, Lawrence G., with Robinson, Patrick, *A Colossal Failure of Common Sense: The Inside Story of the Collapse of Lehman Brothers* (Three Rivers Press, an imprint of the Crown Publishing Group, New York, New York, 2009), p. 1-2.

3. Ibid., p. X.

4. "Rock You Like a Hurricane" by the Scorpions, from the Album, "Love at First Sting," Harvest/EMI and Mercury Records, 1984.

5. O'Connor, Colleen, "Teachers to broach 9/11 carefully, if at all," *The Denver Post*, Sept. 11, 2007.

6. Grossman, Andrew and Reddy, Sumathi, "A More Divided 9/11 Anniversary, *The Wall Street Journal*, September 10, 2010.

7. Associated Press, "Saudi Prince Backs Moving Planned NYC Mosque," October 28, 2010.

8. Ibid.

9. Ibid.

10. Canfield, Jack, *The Success Principles: How to Get from Where You Are to Where You Want to Be.* (New York, NY: HarperCollins Publishers, 2005.)

11. Jeremiah 29:11, NKJV.

CHAPTER 2

DENIAL IS <u>NOT</u> JUST A RIVER IN EGYPT!

I was in my residency as a chaplain in what many of us in the arena know as Clinical Pastoral Education (CPE). This was a saying among us, not so much to be funny, but rather a play on words because most were not acknowledging the reality. In many personal cases, denial followed the diagnosis or death of someone close to them. Dr. Kubler-Ross stated, "Denial functions as a buffer after unexpected shocking news, (and) allows the patient to collect himself and, with time, mobilize other, less radical defenses."[1] I believe God made us this way in order for us to protect ourselves and then process the event or news in a manner and at a rate that will eventually lead to the final place of acceptance where a person can continue with life.

Denial can be like a two-edged sword. We can develop an assumption in our worldview saying, "This could never happen to me." The other edge of the sword comes when the event happens or disaster strikes, causing us to say, "This cannot be happening to me." Whether personally or corporately, we must recognize this step in the processing of grief and loss and tackle it head on if we desire to embrace our future.

THE POWER OF TRUTH

In order to get to that place of acceptance, we must get out of the ditch of denial. The best way to do this is by speaking the truth in love.[2] When someone shares this truth in love, we have less difficulty grasping it because we can tell the person genuinely cares. If we care for people and see them stuck in a ditch, we will naturally assist them to get back on the path called life. Life lived following a time of trauma or grief is referred to as the "new normal," meaning the former way of life is transformed, but now the life ahead of us is what we have. To succeed we will have to make the most of it, realizing the best days can be in the future.

Truth is the ultimate weapon when combating doubt, denial and grief. Pontius Pilate used an opportunity to the fullest potential when he asked Jesus, "What is truth?"[3] He could have asked him anything as the Roman Governor over Israel then, but this is the question he posed. We, as a nation, have had the power of truth sown into the fabric of our foundation, which we perceive in our judicial system. Even in TV shows, we could recite the question simultaneously as someone was taking the stand: "Do you swear to tell the truth, the whole truth, and nothing but the truth, so help you, God?" When it comes to grief, we must embrace the whole truth and nothing but the truth, or we will not continue being constructively present. Let me illustrate this on a personal level and progress up to a national level of how denial has been functioning.

THE DREADED "C" WORD

The power of denial is personal for me. In December, 1998, I was being examined at Ft. Meade VA Hospital outside of Sturgis, SD, for follow up with the Gulf War Syndrome Medical Review. Thankfully I had a doctor who was very thorough and happened to notice a very irregular mole on my back. He invited a specialist to come and take a look at me in order to get an expert as well as second opinion. His first words were, "I want him in my operating room immediately." As one might guess, I was thinking this was impossible because I was still in my 20's and indestructible. I was on swing shift and needed to be at work in a few hours, "What does he mean, "I want him in my operating room immediately"? The surgeon replied, "You have a melanoma skin cancer and I need to remove that as soon as possible."

I admit I was more than likely going into shock at this point and did not know what to say or how to react. However, I do remember denying this was true! I did not go to surgery that day, but scheduled it for ten days later. I also made an appointment with a dermatologist to get an "expert second opinion" to add to the previous expert second opinion. When I heard the dermatologist say he thought it was cancer, I followed through with the surgery. Sure enough, the pathology for that mole came back as a melanoma, but detected very early at only 0.25 mm deep in my skin. I had a basal cell cancer discovered six months later, but did not go through the same process, because my mind was capable of "handling" the information and I had this outpatient surgery on the exact same day without needing the second opinion. This diagnosis led to quarterly follow ups for the next five years and yearly full body exams continue. Even the term "diagnosis" bears significance to the truth. Coming from the Greek word for knowledge with a preposition attached to it, we have this meaning of being "founded in the knowledge or the facts presented." For years, I have been in a position spiritually, mentally and emotionally

I AM IN A POSITION TO HANDLE THE FACTS AND MOVE FORWARD

where I could handle the facts and move forward. Presently, I am going on twelve years without any other occurrences and I am grateful. This personal experience has helped me relate to the cancer patients that I interact with on a daily basis and made me both sympathetic and empathetic for their circumstances and how all of us go through a cyclical pattern of grief. Remember, only our heart knows its own bitterness and only we know when we experience joy.[4]

ALL IN THE FAMILY

Sometimes, an event has an impact on an entire family system—leaving everyone devastated. Since I have daughters, a story grips me and I still pray for the family. When Natalie Holloway disappeared on her senior trip, friends did not know the details, the family became alarmed, and a nation rallied to this case in order to find out what had happened.[5]

Unfortunately, we do have a number of missing persons cases every year, but this one caught everyone's attention.

After drugs and alcohol, then guns, people are the third "commodity" to be trafficked. The movie, *Taken*, brought this whole scenario to light and made people realize this goes beyond Hollywood cinema, but affects millions every year.[6] In the case of Natalie Holloway, billions became aware that she was missing and many people wanted to find out what really happened? In the movie, there is a "partially good" ending in which the father found his daughter still alive and was able to rescue her. However, her friend died along with countless other women who were victims of the trafficking industry.[7] The dad in the movie was motivated not just to save her life, but also had the other underlying agenda to know the truth and be able to move forward in that truth. If we possessed the skills that he did within the movie, I assure you that any dad would have pursued the same quest for truth. Can you capture how important closure is for them?

Eight years later, we still do not have the entire truth of what happened to Natalie. The Holloways do not have the truth about their daughter. However, when the Amanda Berry story broke in Ohio along with the two other women, this story emphasized why truth is so important.[8] Denial can be a powerful force in a good way because we always want to cling to hope. Ultimately, a positive future and a confident expectation are divine goals.[9] Do you see the importance of truth for you?

NOT IN OUR TOWN!

When it comes to our home town or our community, we can deny the very fact that disaster—natural or otherwise—can strike at any time, even repeatedly. Since I was raised in the Dakotas, I have observed some pretty spectacular thunderstorms. The sound of a siren going off issuing a tornado warning sparks an adrenaline rush similar to the one received when in combat. Our assumptions of living in a beautiful, peaceful land get shattered by that rare occurrence that can create terror.

July 5, 1997, was a gorgeous day in Belle Fourche, South Dakota. This was true until that evening. We did not have a tornado touch down that night, though the roar of that storm sounded very familiar to my brother, Mike, and me. The storm gave proof of its potency in the form of 3.5 inch diameter hail lasting for over 20 minutes. Up until that moment we could deny that hail like that could ever happen here. Yet, every roof in town, every car outside, every exposed window was shattered, just like our belief system.

Littleton, Colorado, was a quiet, beautiful suburb until April 20, 1999. Two young men made a choice to interrupt this untouchable thought and place that suburb on the map of everyone's mind. This event was like a rock thrown into a calm lake, the ripples in the water just kept on going. Thirteen years later, the shooting at the Aurora movie theatre proved that those ripples were still there.

New Orleans, as a community, denied that a hurricane would ever become too big or make a direct hit to overcome a barrier. Someone even managed to develop residential communities that were well below the waterline with this assumption. With denial this grand, could this be the reason for the ensuing flood of anger turning into rage? Could this be the epicenter of the overwhelming grief that was experienced?

What about that company or business that provided one third of the jobs in your community and then moves, closes or fails? You may have had three generations serve in that same place, but could the impossible happen? Going back to Lehman Brothers and the landmark it was for 158 years, what do you do if something has that size and history to stop from believing, "That did not happen?" In Belle Fourche, the previous generation still says that about the sugar beet factories.

Whether we realize it or not, we could all name assumptions or certain "denials" we live with because we have made it our normal way of thinking. Many of us could name our personal communities that may still be in denial or disbelief that any such disaster could actually impact us.

ONE NATION, UNTOUCHABLE?

New York is a world-renowned city. Since 1980, I wanted to visit the city because I would watch that ball drop every New Year's Eve. I wanted to see Times Square for myself. I wanted to see where my dad's parents came through on Ellis Island in 1924. I never imagined a plane flying into the World Trade Center, let alone two. I never perceived that I would see New York for more than ten hours on TV on September 11, 2001. What do New Yorkers feel? What do you feel? What does our nation feel?

We had seen conflict, but not on our own soil since Pearl Harbor. As a nation, were we in denial that something could actually happen here, domestically? Did we come to the point where we thought we were untouchable again? We were certainly in denial and disbelief with the shock and awe the first day. Unless you were there or at the Pentagon, or working on the airlines that day, or managed to get around a TV with the news reporting it live, it was easy to think someone made up the story.

AN EYE WITNESS ACCOUNT

Terri just happened to be on vacation, seeing the great city of New York on September 11, 2001. She, her mom, and one other person were near "Ground Zero" already that morning when life dramatically changed for them.[10]

Terri was only a few blocks away when this commotion started. She managed to capture some photos of the second plane hitting the second tower.[11] She caught the smoke coming out of the side of the building that

seemed to form a devilish face.[12] That picture alone spoke more than a thousand words and made me want to speak with a chaplain! I asked her if she had heard any explosions on the ground, because I had already read about certain conspiracy theories. Terri had not heard anything prior to the World Trade Center collapsing. Shock, awe, disbelief and denial engulfed the multitude along with the dust cloud. The anger, depression and despair soon followed and lingered like the smoldering rubble.

WHAT ABOUT THE 9/11 COMMISSION?

President George W. Bush and the U. S. Congress established the "9/11 Commission" by law in order to answer numerous questions as well as provide a plan of action.[13] This work had the best of intentions and came up with hundreds of pages in background, research, analysis and action plans, but it still left me asking questions. I am not alone, because I was in denial along with countless other Americans, even foreigners, thinking that the truth is eluding us here.

WHAT ABOUT OMISSIONS AND DISTORTIONS?[14]

Proving that I was not alone, this is where the conspiracy theories and a plethora of literary works appeared, because that is what happens when we are in denial. We will try to come to our own conclusions without the whole truth. We will also do some digging of our own, it is in our nature. Just consider Roswell or the JFK assassination as examples that still breed theories because of a lack of closure. Mr. Griffin did do some great digging and brings up many points that one would think they would have mentioned in the original 9/11 Commission Report.[15] I must say that I am still not convinced of the truth because too many mysteries remain.

WHAT ABOUT NECESSARY SECRETS?

Having worked in the Intelligence Community, I can reassure you that some secrets cannot be shared. Their exposure in "real" time would cause far more damage than the truth itself. Mr. Schoenfeld did a great job of proving this to be the case from a historical foundation that goes back to our nation's inception.[16] Most of the secrets are kept for our own sanity and protection. However, from a chaplain's perspective, some necessary truths filling the gaping wounds of grief would bring healing and provide comfort to those who lost loved ones, livelihoods, and lifestyles. What do you think those truths might be?

WHAT IS MY PERSPECTIVE?

I would want to have the right team in place with one goal in mind: the truth. The 9/11 Commission that I would have picked would have been experts within the Intelligence, Surveillance, and Reconnaissance (ISR) field who know how to find answers as well as retrieve those answers. I would want to have some scientists, engineers, pilots, and Air Traffic Controllers (ATC's) that could prove or disprove what the evidence presented. I would have a couple attorneys on staff to file for subpoenas in order to get the legal access to information. My friend, whom I will call "Bob," would be the person to go to concerning cultural and religious aspects. Having been raised in the Middle East, he speaks 52 dialects of Arabic, has the Quran memorized, and received his education at Oxford. Then I would have three at the top of the ISR field who know how to put the pieces together and let them give the full picture.

The black boxes to all four planes would stop every conspiracy theory because we would know who controlled the four planes, not just one. If we had those pieces of information, then it would prove who to blame, whether a decade (plus) of conflict was just or not, who we must forgive (or ask for forgiveness), and clarify our path for the future. Obviously, we would like as much of the truth as possible, because it would disarm the denial with one mighty blow.

DENIAL, THE TWO-EDGED SWORD

Denial can be like a two-edged sword. We can develop an assumption in our worldview saying, "This could never happen to me (us)." The other edge of the sword comes when the event happens or disaster strikes, causing us to say, "This cannot be happening." Whether personally or corporately, we must recognize this step in the processing of grief and loss and tackle it head on if we desire to embrace our future.

When it comes to 9/11, all these years later, denial, misunderstanding, BS (once again, this is Blame-Shifting), and conspiracy theories abound. I have been reading and researching for six years and I am amazed at what is out there. Furthermore, we are left hanging with more questions anytime we start digging for the truth, because the truth has eluded us. If we want to get on the path of life again, we will need denial to be trumped with the truth.

CASE STUDY: THE PRESIDENTIAL ELECTION IN THE UNITED STATES

Let's look at the Presidential elections. We have people in denial or shock because of who was elected. Due to fraud, computer hacking or programming, illegal voters, dead voters, or corrupt counters, the person we thought won did not win. I know what you may be thinking, but do you remember the year 2000? The election came down to one county in Florida by 300 votes. People were screaming in outrage that there was voter fraud and the Supreme Court made the call, but former Vice President Al Gore conceded unwillingly, probably with millions of Americans in his wake. The election in 2012 was not a new feeling, just for a different group of people. I believe our nation has had millions of people stuck in denial for years and history seems to be repeating itself once again. What if we could eliminate the denial?

From a chaplain's or counselor's perspective, getting a client to cycle through grief to the level of acceptance becomes much easier when the truth comes out. In the area of elections within the United States, we have the ability to assure a fair, accountable election, but those parameters have not been put in place. I also know that most politicians are not chaplains or counselors, but my point is that we should care about where we are and where we go as a nation. In many facets of life, whether on a personal level or national level, truth has a way of combating denial like nothing else.

Samuel Taylor Coleridge said it well:

"If men could learn from history, what lessons it might teach us! But passion and party blind our eyes, and the light which experience gives is a lantern on the stern, which shines only on the waves behind us!"[17]

DO ALL ROADS LEAD TO ROME?

Rome and the Roman civilization still speak in the lessons of many areas of life. The roads that lead to and from Rome still go out like the spokes on a wheel. What event or events in your life keep bringing you back to the same place? Like the fire that broke out and consumed much of ancient Rome in A.D. 64, did you BS about that event or keep getting snagged into that ditch repeatedly or even distort the truth or lie about it?

In life, many of us have had that place where we do keep getting stuck. I want us to get out of that ditch and have the humility to receive the help if we need it. As a nation, I believe we have been stuck since 9/11, perhaps beyond in some cases. I will even explore that in greater detail a little bit later. I believe every human heart truly longs to be free, and freedom is sown in the fabric of our nation, in its very foundation. The truth is what makes us free.[18] Are you willing to explore the truth? Are you willing to be free? Then I challenge you to embrace the journey and begin.

QUESTIONS TO CONSIDER

1. Do you recognize denial in your life? In your business? In your community? In your nation?

2. What are the one or two areas you are presently focused on?

3. What do you feel?

4. What is the truth or facts that you need?

5. Do you need an expert second opinion to the last expert second opinion?

6. What if we could eliminate the denial? What would that look like?

7. How willing are you to find freedom? What would that look like for you?

Endnotes

1. Kubler-Ross, *On Death and Dying,* p. 52.

2. Ephesians 4:15, NKJV.

3. John 18:38, NASB.

4. Proverbs 14:10, NKJB, paraphrase mine.

5. Geraldo Rivera, "The Natalie Holloway Case," *The Geraldo Rivera Show,* Fox News, June 20, 2005.

6. *Taken,* Twentieth Century Fox, 2009.

7. Ibid.

8. Sheeran, Thomas J. "Amanda Berry, Gina DeJesus and Michelle Knight: Victims Of Ohio Kidnap Case Break Their Silence" The Huffington Post, July 9, 2013.

9. Jeremiah 29:11, NKJV.

10. Jensen, Wade, Terri Spitzer Personal Interview, April 17, 2011.

11. Terri Spitzer's photographs provided were off by one day because of the program being off for Leap year.

12. Ibid.

13. The 9/11 Commission Report: Final Report of the National Commission on Terrorist Attacks Upon the United States, Authorized Edition (New York, NY: W. W. Norton & Company, 2004)

14. Griffin, David Ray, *The 9/11 Commission Report: Omissions and Distortions* (Northampton, MA: Olive Branch Press, 2005).

15. Ibid.

16. Schoenfeld, Gabriel, *Necessary Secrets: National Security, the Media, and the Rule of Law* (New York, NY: W.W. Norton and Company, 2010.

17. The Oxford Dictionary of Quotations, Third Edition, Samuel Taylor Coleridge, December 18, 1831 (Oxford University Press, 1979), p. 157: 20.

18. John 8:32, NKJV, paraphrase mine.

CHAPTER 3

IS ANGER RIGHTEOUS OR RAVENOUS?

If there is any emotion or feeling that is accepted in any culture, this is it! We do not have to look hard to see anger manifested around the world from every tribe, ethnic group and nation. Among the Danish and German sides of my family, men were noted either for their temper or their anger issues. However, could that not be said for all of us? When it comes to the grief and loss cycle, anger has no problem proving that it is part of the process.

Some people feel that they have a righteous indignation when it comes to their anger. After all, if an injustice led to the grief or loss, then aren't we entitled to have anger flow through the veins? Depending on how great the loss is, which is dependent on the perception of the people going through it, the anger can also carry an entitlement of time with it. Have you ever felt licensed to hold on to your anger and allow it to grow, even if it affected others around you?

Some people allow anger to fester so that it becomes ravenous and eats at their soul. This is where righteous indignation has turned to spiritual indigestion, disrupting us at the very core of our being. If this ravenous anger is left untreated, it becomes cancerous to our soul and consumes us. How do we know when we have crossed the line? If we look like a Marine who ate rusty nails for dinner and washed it down with turpentine, chances are very high that we have allowed the anger to go too far. Have we been around someone like that? Could that person be you?

THE RED DOT

To say I was surprised when I found out I was one of them would be a complete understatement. I had signed up to go to a men's retreat and was thinking it might just be another one of those to pump me up. I had to fill out some paperwork about myself and be somewhat self-disclosing with the other participants before I went. When I was being brought in and going through the registration process, each of us were taken to a quiet corner where a counselor sat down with us. My counselor went through my paperwork and said I would receive a red dot because I was dealing with anger. I almost shouted, "No, I'm not!"

As one might guess, I was even shocked at what came out of me. I did not mention anything in the paperwork, but the anger had been festering for five years and he could see it, along with my wife and countless others around me. I just could not see it because it had become a part of me.

Five years prior to this men's retreat, I had a minister and elder publicly humiliate me, and, in my opinion, betray me. According to my perception, I lost a mentor, a friend, a mutual trust, and credibility with dozens that were around to witness this. The loss was horrendous, and the anger was overwhelming. During that men's retreat, all of that anger came out like Mt. St. Helens erupting on the inside of me. I am not the world's biggest or strongest guy at 5 feet, 8 inches, so I was literally amazed I broke a medicine ball, releasing all of the fury that had built up over five years. Wouldn't forgiveness have been so much easier? The answer is emphatically yes! I will discuss that later. For now let's take that fury to another level beyond the individual.

THE FAMILY'S FURY ALONG WITH HIS FRIENDS

My brother Mike and I roomed together with Brandon in his townhouse during my last eighteen months of college. We were like the "Three Amigos" who would not let our classes interfere with our college education.[1] We still received good grades, but had a network of friends at the University of Wyoming that crossed every type of group at the school. One of those friends we had in common was John. John was this charismatic guy everyone liked, who also happened to be one of the best builders of speaker systems for your car if you wanted to go thumping down the road. One night, not different from many others, we stayed up late watching movies, visiting, and eating pizza, so John spent the night at the townhouse.

The following morning, we said goodbye to John and said that we would see him later because he was going to help Mike and Brandon install a speaker system. John never made it back. We did not know he spent his last night on earth with us. Since the man was convicted, I can say John was murdered that day for no reason other than hate. In utter horror, John's parents lost their son, we lost a great friend, and the college community lost an outstanding example as a student. The man guilty of this murder received life in prison, but he would not even have his life if the police had not apprehended him before the family's fury or ours had gotten to him first. Our anger toward the person responsible enboldened us to enact good old-fashioned Wyoming prairie justice, and the injustice of this occurrence could have choked him—like Darth Vader using the Force.[2]

LEHMAN, NOW I KNOW

Another way to get people angry is by hitting them in their "wallet," which may refer to their jobs, accounts, retirement plans, or investments. When we have a loss of our identity in a job or title as well as the financial loss of everything that we worked for up to that point, the grief manifesting in the form of anger can be tumultuous. How do we deal with such overwhelming fury that originates from one single event?

Once again, I would like to share Mr. McDonald's experience of walking by the occupied "Lehman Brothers" building:

"I suppose in a sense, I had seen only its demise, the four-year death rattle of twenty-first century finance, which ended on September 15, 2008. Yet, in my mind, I remember the great days. And as I come to a halt outside the building, I know too that the next few moments will be engulfed by sadness. But I always stop ...

Swamped by nostalgia, edged as we all are by a lingering anger, and still plagued by unanswerable questions, I stand and stare upward, sorrowful beyond reason, and trapped by the twin words of those possessed of flawless hindsight: *if only*."[3]

If we just stopped on this date, the "lingering anger" Mr. McDonald feels along with all of the Lehman Brothers employees, not to mention customers, we would have a surge of anger that would be like lightning looking for somewhere to strike. It wouldn't just stop with a "boss" like Mr. Richard Fuld, "who seemed to have lost touch with the times as well as with his people."[4] Just as lightning will strike at random, it is still drawn to certain objects that are metallic or standing out higher than others. Anger, in relation to loss, can be the same way. The loss is real, at times catastrophic, and the anger manifesting following this is legitimate.

The loss did not just stop here at Lehman Brothers. On September 29, 2008, the market dropped 777.7 points, and what a number to stop on! At this point, the loss was global and trillions of dollars literally vaporized within these two weeks. I knew who Lehman Brothers was as a company, and I was mad at the company as well as the government for making choices of who to bail out. I was angry at a system that allows retirement accounts to be unprotected. I was angry at a nation for allowing bad loans to be given out in the first place. I was angry at the depraved human traits, which allow greed to consume everyone and everything in its wake. These are some "random strikes" that I propelled, but what or who has your anger "struck down" on? Have you or your business been the root of some unforeseen loss?

THE OUTRAGE
OF A COMMUNITY

Since I lived near historic, downtown Littleton for years, I can still focus on that fateful day in 1999. This community still has outrage over the Columbine High School shooting. When it comes to an act like this, it is ultimately the perpetrators' personal responsibility and their choices that murdered the students and teacher. Yet, the anger of the community was so great that the parents of those boys had to move. One dad was a doctor who had to sell his practice and move out of the state and the other dad was a retired Master Sergeant from the United States Air Force. I consider both of these dads as outstanding citizens. However, the anger of the community became charged and they were the "lightning rods" that received the brunt of the anger and the outcry.

I said before that when it comes to grief and loss, when another event occurs, the result is not simply adding to the load, it multiplies and becomes an exponential burden. In July, 2012, the shooting at the Aurora theatre, another suburb in the Denver area, caused an outrage with political repercussions. Many people could still remember the Columbine shooting like it was yesterday and all the weight of their outrage and anguish was compounded. In my opinion, gun owners and the gun industry were the lightning rod for people's anger, because it is just easier than pointing the finger at ourselves and taking personal responsibility. Look at our culture. We have a general disrespect for life, producing fruit we do not want to eat. Yet, we are the ones who have planted the seeds. Are we blaming others or taking our anger out on others who do not deserve it? How angry are you? Sometimes a righteous anger must arise that leads to the truth and a genuine change, but the other kind is ravenous and causes more destruction, both inwardly and outwardly.

When it came to a natural disaster in our nation, I have not seen anything get coverage in our media like Hurricane Katrina. Thousands of people had their lives turned upside down. The documented anger turning to rage captured me more than anything. Blame shifting accompanied the anger, which was another way of the people letting their anger strike where it may. Numerous people or organizations were blamed for this disaster, even President George W. Bush, but as far as I know, no person can control the weather. In recent history, the only person to believe that a person could influence the weather was General Patton accrediting his chaplain for making a weather prayer that shifted the conditions and the battlefront in World War II.

The anger grew so intense that martial law had to be declared in areas struck by the hurricane. Friends of mine, both military and civilian, were entrenched in Southern Mississippi and Louisiana. They had not seen anything like this, not even in a war zone. Comments made by local officials hindered the situation rather than helped it, emblazoning the wrath. If anger does go unchecked any of us could become as volatile as nitroglycerin and destroy anything around us, even our loved ones and neighbors. Make no mistake, this is the worst place to be stuck in the grieving process. How do we get out of this death spiral? You will soon see, but you can seldom do it alone.

"FROM HELL'S HEART, I STAB AT THEE!"[5]

Just one month after 9/11, my wife and I went to a conference in Toronto, Ontario, Canada. People were there from around the world and America had their sympathy. Then there was a shift. President Kennedy once said, "we would pay any price and attack any foe who threatened our liberty,"[6] and the demand for justice had swiftly gone out. The denial in our nation had turned to anger and numerous people wanted to get the ones who were responsible for the attacks. The war cry of our nation was perceived as a wounded, domesticated animal lashing out at anything coming within close proximity.

Whether we were justified or not, only 100% of the truth revealed would make the rest of the world think more highly of us. When we invaded Iraq in 2003, many nations thought we were like a bully who had his nose bloodied, and now we were out for vengeance. Although we were not on our last breath, only Ricardo Montalban as Kahn could have quoted Shakespeare with such indignation and eloquence that his decree seemed to be that of our own nation, "From hell's heart, I stab at thee."[7]

Whatever perception there was, I have no doubt that our mainstream media picked up on this tone and turned against the Bush Administration as well as the military. The anger had turned to blame shifting and to this day, much of it is still unresolved. The anger even turned inward when there was a highlight of the body count in Iraq rather than the pursuit of a foe and the liberty of another nation that was extremely honored to have us in their nation. Military members follow orders given by civilians and 99.9 % serve honorably. The anger was turned inward with the military by the actual results of their efforts not being told. This statue dedicated to the military servicemen and women represents the sacrifice that many gave: everything. The only one recognizing the price paid along with the member is an Iraqi girl.[8]

As a nation, we have been stuck in this anger for far too long. We are our own worst enemy because we are spiritually and morally divided. A nation divided against itself will not stand.[9] We must deal with the anger now before it does consume us because history has proven civilizations can crumble. Our anger has become ravenous rather than righteous. What do you think we can do as a nation?

YOU MEAN ANGER IS OK?

Whether as an individual, a business, a community or a nation, I want you to grasp a few things. We can be angry, but not miss the mark.[10] How do I know this? According to Scripture, God became angry![11] If God is a holy God and cannot sin and He became angry, then it is alright for us to be angry as well. As mentioned, anger is a natural step in our cycling through the grieving process. We were given this in order to ultimately lead to acceptance and healing. We can be righteous, or have a right to be angry. If we have suffered loss, or injustice, or both, we can and will be angry about it.

We run into trouble when we let the "sun go down on our anger."[12] Furthermore, the apostle Paul wrote, "Let all bitterness, wrath, anger, clamor and slander be put away from you, along with all malice."[13] As I have heard many times, bitterness is like drinking poison and hoping the other person dies. If you want to know what ravenous anger looks like, this is a good summary. Do you have anger that looks like this? If so, let go of it before you turn to the dark side. Chances are that you will need assistance in this and that is where we are headed. Take courage, if I can do it, then so can you. We can deal with our anger, but it will take truth and tough choices. What kind of choices are you willing to make in order to break free?

QUESTIONS TO CONSIDER

1. Have you ever felt entitled to hold on to your anger and allow it to grow, affecting others around you?

2. Have you been able to tell when you are around someone, or several people who have let their anger go too far? Could that person be you?

3. Who has your anger been directed towards?

4. Have you or your business been the root of some unforeseen loss?

5. Can you identify an area of loss in your community that people are still angry about?

6. Do you have anger that looks ravenous?

7. What do you think we can do as a nation to become free from unresolved anger resulting from injustice?

8. What kind of choices are you willing to make in order to break free?

Endnotes

1. "I have never let my schooling interfere with my education." This quote is attributed to Mark Twain in 1907.

2. *Star Wars,* Lucas Films, 1977.

3. McDonald, Lawrence G., with Robinson, Patrick, *A Colossal Failure of Common Sense: The Inside Story of the Collapse of Lehman Brothers* (Three

Rivers Press, an imprint of the Crown Publishing Group, New York, New York, 2009), p. 1-2.

4. Ibid. p. 300.

5. *Star Trek II, The Wrath of Kahn*, 1982.

6. Kennedy, John F., Inaugural Address, January 20, 1961.

7. Star Trek II, *The Wrath of Kahn*, 1982

8. Kibbey, Benjamin R., *Changing Faces: Statue Honors Fallen Heroes*, Army News Service, January 6, 2004. Retrieved from: http://web.archive.org/web/20040622080707/http://www4.army.mil/ocpa/read.php?story_id_key=5563.

9. Matthew 12:25, NKJV.

10. Ephesians 4:26, NKJV, but my paraphrase of what sin means, "to miss the mark."

11. Isaiah 47:6 and Zecharia 1:2 are just two out of several references (NKJV).

12. Ephesians 4:26, NKJV.

13. Ephesians 4:31, NKJV.

CHAPTER 4

TO BARGAIN OR NOT TO BARGAIN?

We are looking for all kinds of bargains in the United States, but I do not think this is what many of us had in mind. However, the kind of bargaining I am speaking about occurs with uncanny regularity in our culture, whether in books, media, or the people around us, not to mention ourselves. This step in the grieving process may not be as pronounced in many people, but it does manifest itself with the "what if" questions. If you wonder why a chaplain may recognize this, often times someone asks, "Why did God let this happen?" or "Where was God when all of this was going on?"

In my personal journey when I had the diagnosis confirmed of melanoma., I asked them all. I asked the big "God" questions for sure, but I also asked the simple ones. What if I had more of my mom's genes rather than my dad's? My dad is full Danish and a red-head, whose skin I happened to inherit. Due to a number of issues from the Gulf War (Desert Shield/Desert Storm), what if this was caused by something there? It was in a conspicuous place on my back and knowing the results of fair skin, I used sunblock profusely. I was burned as a kid a few times due to being at a lake and thinking about fishing rather than the sun, but what if I had not been burned those few times? My dad was burned several hundred times and did not end up with melanoma, so why did I? What is the bargaining question presently going through your mind?

Skin cancer was just one event in my life, which generated scores of questions throughout the grieving process. Yet, this occurs in every form of loss that we encounter. As the loss is magnified, the questions get magnified along with it. We truly do want the answers to these questions, but they do not always come so quickly or easily. Once again, truth plays a critical role in getting through this stage, just as it does with denial. The more "bargaining chips" or questions we eliminate, the faster we move toward acceptance. What "bargaining chips" do you need to place on the table?

WHAT IF I?

Terri Spitzer is already a pretty amazing person in my book, having overcome childhood cancer. The Cobalt radiation used when she was a child is the reason that I met her along with her mother Beryl. Amazingly, these circumstances are not the ones that give her post traumatic issues. To this day, the sound of a plane or the thought of flying do not leave a positive feeling for Terri. Seeing New York was a childhood dream, but "just happening to be in New York" near the World Trade Center turned into a nightmare for her.[1]

Terri had been to New York three previous times, so they had a hotel off 34th Street which had become their landing pad, giving them access to the Subway and the rest of Manhattan. On this trip her nephew was with her as well as her mother. They were advised by her cousin to go to the Statue of Liberty first, then the Empire State Building, and finally to visit the Twin Towers. All three were close to the boat dock on the morning of September 11, 2001. They heard a loud crash, but could not see through the trees. Then someone said a plane had hit the World Trade Center. When Terri, Beryl, and her nephew were at a place to see, that is when the second plane hit and she was able to get these pictures.[2]

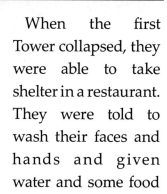

When the first Tower collapsed, they were able to take shelter in a restaurant. They were told to wash their faces and hands and given water and some food when they came out. They did get on a ferry, but did not make it back to their hotel. The ferry took them to New Jersey where they, along with a number of others were taken to an Army post to receive food, clothing and shelter. Here are some pictures taken from the ferry.

A McDonald's had cooked up all the food they had on the premises and brought it to the post. Due to the airport and the city being basically shut down, Terri's sister from North Carolina drove to New Jersey to pick them up and get them back to Colorado another way. These events triggered so much, and left so much lingering besides the luggage in the hotel.

The questions seemed to have little hooks in time. We can be stuck in that moment of time with the questions concerning that instant of loss, perceived or genuine. Perhaps like Terri, you were there on that day and may ask, "Why did it have to be this day? What if we had been somewhere else? What if God would have intervened? What if our family would have gone somewhere else? Myriads of questions can keep coming up like a babbling brook. Do the bargaining questions have hooks in time for you?

WHY WAS THIS OUR FAMILY?

What if our family had been in a different place or a different time? Have you ever heard this question before? After the shock of the event, the denial, and the anger, bargaining will fit right in like a cushion on the couch, but the thoughts are not comfortable. When it came to the Holloway case, similar questions arose.[3] Why did they have to choose our daughter? Why did her friends lose track of her? How did the Dutch man get involved? Was he following her from the time she landed in Aruba? Why were authorities not more thorough?

These questions will drive us to seek the answers, even if the answers are elusive. As a father, I would have flown to Aruba myself to go looking for the answers just as Natalie's father went looking for her along with the answers. In many cases of loss involving a person, we are seeking more than the person or the answers. We are seeking justice. We may not always get any, but when we get all three, this is why there is such joy and satisfaction along with the acceptance. Is justice something we all seek in our situation?

In *Taken*, Bryan Mills, had "a set of very particular skills"[4] that enabled him to not only follow the clues and answer his questions, but also find his daughter and achieve some sense of justice by eliminating the people who perpetrated the crime.[5] Most of us do not have this luxury. We have laws and we cannot just go out to hunt and kill those causing the destruction. This was a movie, after all. But why did this movie do so well? The movie touched our hearts and made us live vicariously through Bryan Mills as he retrieved his daughter alive and relatively unharmed. We long for justice, even if only in fantasy.

WE LONG FOR JUSTICE, EVEN IF ONLY IN FANTASY

Amanda Berry, Gina DeJesus and Michelle Knight had been missing for years and were thought to be dead. When a man came to the rescue of these three women enslaved in a quiet, suburban house in Ohio, no one had a clue what was happening.[6] They were found alive a few miles from where they had been taken in Cleveland.[7] The best possible hope of the families came to pass. One big mystery was solved that day, but the bargaining questions began as I considered their situation, their loss. How can you make up for eight to ten years of time? How do you forgive someone who enslaved you and abused you? Why did people, including authorities, not dig deeper in their curiosity when odd things were observed over the years? Why did this have to be their family? As family, how do you support these young ladies to embrace life along with reconciliation?

WAS IT YOUR MOVE OR MINE?

Have you or someone you love moved with the company and just settled in, only to find out that they are being laid off due to the economy, downsized? Maybe your company completely disappeared in one night? This phenomenon is not just Lehman Brothers. Do you remember the "Dot Bombs?" These ".coms," such as Worldcom, were internet-based companies receiving unwarranted hype and millions of dollars from eager investors, but ending in failure with the funds being incinerated and investors left with empty pockets.

Numerous companies like this sprang up like weeds, and then seemed to be pulled up and tossed away as quickly as they grew. Even in the military we have not been exempt from this. I have numerous friends who received their permanent change of station (PCS), which is a transfer in civilian language. Upon making the PCS, thousands of military members were given termination orders, thanking them for their service to their country. Personnel, both enlisted and officer, saw terminations happen within just a few years of retirement. United Airlines pilots saw their pensions get wiped out regardless of years of service.

Since 9/11, the service industry including hotels, airlines, travel agencies, restaurants, and cruise lines became like the March Madness brackets that my roommate would make in college, to see who was still remaining. This analogy is the same in the financial services industry and department stores. You can pick your line of work. Here are some common questions I have heard. Why did I choose this area? What if I would have chosen another company or branch of service? Is this where I was called to be? God, was this a mistake? Was I in the will of God? Was this hardship in the will of God? What other questions have you asked in bargaining your way through?

WHY NOT THEIR TOWN? THIS IS NOTHING NEW!

New Orleans is one of those cities that I knocked off my bucket list in 1989. I had a desire to see a city that was rich in culture and history. For a relatively young nation, New Orleans is one of the older cities, being founded in 1718. The French Quarter, the architecture with the French influence, and the Café Du Monde were some highlights for me.

Historically, this city has great significance for our nation, but so do the hurricanes for this city and region. Dozens of hurricanes have hit the Mississippi River Basin alone. After so many hurricanes, why do people stay? They stay for the same reason that you and I stay in our respective cities and communities. We are familiar with it and used to it, but we also grow to love the city we make our dwelling. We may also have familial and financial ties to the area. But the question may be, "How many hurricanes classified as Category 3 or higher (the "Big Cats") must we have come through here?" According to historical records for New Orleans, the city is hit about once a decade.[8]

If we become used to the patterns, we can become complacent, or slip back into complete denial that a storm "like that" could come through and hit us again. Grief can also make us numb to the events, even dangers around us. I may repeat this several times to make this point sink in, but grief is exponential in its affect, not just additional. By the previous statistic, a person's age in New Orleans will tell us how many big hurricanes they have seen, survived, and grieved, or continue to grieve.

> GRIEF CAN MAKE US NUMB TO THE EVENTS, EVEN DANGERS AROUND US

With recurring hurricanes, why were we not better prepared to evacuate? Why were we building below sea level? Why were the dykes not thirty feet high with a history of hurricanes surging over twenty feet?[9] Why did gas prices surge the way they did? Why did people assume the government would come to the rescue immediately? I still have my own questions, but I do not live in Louisiana or Mississippi, so I am certain residents from there would have more specific questions of their own.

New York was another city on the bucket list. I have some roots to New York since my dad's parents came to the United States through Ellis Island in 1924. When I was finished with my Army enlistment, I went on a three week trek. One week of that trip was in New York and on Long Island. Coming from rural country, I was fascinated by the "Big Apple." Out of any city in the world, New York is well known for the history, culture, food, entertainment, "never sleeping," Times Square, Central Park, and, of course, the magnificent skyline.

There was something about the skyline that left me captivated, which is also recognizable by many people around the world. My friend, Bryan, took me with him into downtown Manhattan, and I was mesmerized by being in a building on the 52nd floor and looking down. The tallest building I had set foot in prior to this was fifteen stories! I loved the food, enjoyed the nightlife, and was fascinated with the diversity and beauty of the people. New York had been attacked in the past, besides the 1993 failed bombing attempt on the World Trade Center.

Why would anyone want to destroy such a culturally rich, diverse, and exciting city? What if fighter jets would have intercepted those planes? Why did the passengers in the other three planes not revolt against the pilots and hijackers, whoever they were? Where was God in the midst of all of this? Judging by one of the pictures, I do not believe God is the one to blame on this one.[10] To quote a character known as "The Church Lady" coming live from New York, *Saturday Night Live*, "Could it be ... Satan?"

Why would New York be the target again? In 2010, thanks to a veteran recognizing a threat, a bomb that was set to go off near Times Square was thwarted.[11] Now I am doing the blame-shifting, but this does happen in the grieving process as we have already learned. The questions continue to spark something in us and our response can lead us in a number of directions.[12] Keep that in mind as we dream together.

WHAT ABOUT
THE AMERICAN DREAM?

Our family has realized part of the American dream. Considering that my dad's parents came from Denmark with nothing, I am keenly aware that this country provides opportunity like no other. My grandparents worked on building the railroad in western Wyoming, were sharecroppers in Dubois, Wyoming, and finally settled in Riverton where my grandpa became a butcher. The little cabin they called home with three sons was smaller than most people's living rooms are today. They were able to make a good life with what they had. Coming to the United States and finding a new home and a new way of life is still part of the American Dream.

When I was a teenager, I would dream of what life would be like as an adult. I learned to drive in my dad's 1956 Chevy Stepside Truck. Like many men, I not only dreamed of having a sports car, but I wanted my children to be able to drive it when they were in high school. I wanted to be able to do what I enjoyed, and get paid for it. I wanted to be able to learn, to travel, and provide for my children's future. I desired a good life like most other people because of what this nation had as its most valued treasure: opportunity and freedom.

In the United States, we are not told what we will do for a living, we can choose it. My parents had six of us kids, so we did not get every want we desired. However, they instilled great values in us like faith, working hard, personal responsibility, integrity, and perseverance. Thanks to these values and the opportunity this nation provides, five of us siblings graduated with our Bachelor's degree from the University of Wyoming. Three of us have earned a graduate degree. Two of us currently serve in the military. None of us are unemployed. The amazing aspect about this nation is a storyline like this exists in numerous families who can trace back to their ancestors risking it all for their future generations to have opportunity along with freedom. What is your "American Dream?"

We can have all kinds of assumptions along with our questions, but the answers can shatter both of them if it is the answer we did not want. The first car I bought was a 1965 Plymouth Barracuda in 1988. I thought I would hold on to that car until my children entered high school. I honestly never pictured gas going over $4/gallon. The dream I had from childhood was removed.

When it comes to opportunity and freedom, what do we have? I used to love traveling, but not anymore. We have some sense of security, but we have given up the freedom of mobility. We have laws for privacy, but have given up privacy. What if we had not compromised on our foundational values? What if we could go back to our foundational values? Once again, what if our response would have yielded a different outcome, an outcome in which dreams would be kept alive?

BOUNCING BACK AND FORTH

Have these questions made you deny that this really happened again? Or did questions come with the answer you were not looking for? Did the answer make you angry or depressed? This is what I am spelling out in words (see diagram below). The bargaining stage may not be as apparent, but it is legitimate. This is the one stage, more than any other, which can cause us to go all over like a ping pong ball.

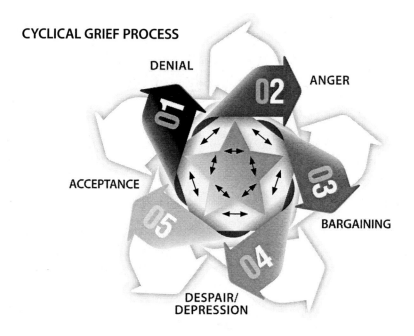

CYCLICAL GRIEF PROCESS

DENIAL

ANGER

ACCEPTANCE

BARGAINING

DESPAIR/ DEPRESSION

Here is the good news, though. Some people can come to the right answer to the bargaining question in their minds and move forward in the cycle. The art, more than the science, is realizing where the questions are taking you in your grieving process.

As a nation, we still have far too many questions left unanswered at this point in time. Perhaps we have not yet asked all the right questions. Regardless of our affiliation, we can make an assessment of where we are and determine where we want to be based on our identity as a nation. The "American Dream" is not dead, but must be defined once again, be reawakened, and another be realized by all of us. Hopefully, we can resolve these questions and move forward together.

QUESTIONS TO CONSIDER

1. What is the bargaining question presently going through your mind?

2. What "bargaining chips" do you need to place on the table?

3. Do the bargaining questions have hooks in time for you?

4. Is justice something we all seek in our situation?

5. How do we embrace life along with reconciliation after experiencing loss?

6. Were you in the will of God?

7. Where was God when you were experiencing your loss? Did you see God at work in your favor?

8. What is your "American Dream?"

9. What if our response would have yielded a different outcome, an outcome in which dreams would be kept alive?

10. Did you notice if the questions moved you to denial, anger, depression or acceptance?

Endnotes

1. Wade Jensen, Terri Spitzer Interview, April 17, 2011. The entire "What if I?" section is based off her interview.

2. Photographs taken by Terri Spitzer on September 11, 2001.

3. Geraldo Rivera, "The Natalie Holloway Case," *The Geraldo Rivera Show*, Fox News, June 20, 2005.

4. *Taken*, 20th Century Fox, 2009.

5. Ibid.

6. Coyne, John, and Sheeran, Thomas J., *Amanda Berry, Gina DeJesus Found Alive In Ohio After Being Reported Missing For 10 Years*, Huffington Post, May 6, 2013.

7. Ibid.

8. http://web.mit.edu/12.000/www/m2010/finalwebsite/background/hurricanes/history.html, accessed August 14, 2013.

9. Ibid.

10. See the photo with the smoke in the form of a demonic face taken by Terry Spitzer shown at the bottom left of page 45.

11. Candiotti, Susan, and Jeanne Meserve, *Car Bomb Found in Parked SUV in Times Square*, CNN, May 2, 2010

12. http://www.cnn.com/2010/CRIME/05/02/times.square.closure/index.html , accessed August 15, 2013.

WE WERE PROMISED
SUFFERINGS. THEY WERE
PART OF THE PROGRAM.
WE WERE EVEN TOLD,
"BLESSED ARE THEY THAT
MOURN," AND I ACCEPT
IT. I'VE GOT NOTHING
THAT I HADN'T
BARGAINED FOR. OF
COURSE IT IS DIFFERENT
WHEN THE THING
HAPPENS TO ONESELF,
NOT TO OTHERS,
AND IN REALITY, NOT
IMAGINATION."

—C.S. LEWIS

CHAPTER 5

1959, AN ARBITRARY YEAR[1]

In order to demonstrate how the grieving process works and has been working since the dawn of humankind, I picked a moment in time that may seem arbitrary, but is intentional. This was the year that my dad graduated from high school. My dad has talked about this time in his life more than any other. Therefore, I actually conducted an interview with him so I could have his perspective as well as a historical one.[2] For the United States, this was a glorious time.

A GOLDEN AGE

The "Nifty Fifties" are a time my father's generation can relate to when it comes to music, entertainment, cars, night life, travel, business, family, community, and government. Following WWII, many men who served came back with a renewed zest for life along with a distinct purpose to make a future for themselves as well as others. We had not only entered the "Atomic Age," we had also entered a new economic era that had now become global.

Thanks to this new economic age, every other facet of society was impacted. The innovation that came along with this time transformed our way of life as well as society to this present day. My dad remembers when the "TV" became popular. With the use of TV, entertainment and media entered the household, which exponentially expanded these two industries. Think of how important sports has become since the TV expansion! We not only could see the local high school games, but we could also see every professional sport. The Olympics were broadcast before the 1950's, but it was given a worldwide audience in this decade.

The economy within the U. S. was at a state where a man could make a living working at a gas station and be able to support a family, yet it was opportunistic for any person to start a business and see it excel due to a balance between the cost of living and earning a living. Companies and corporations rewarded people for their loyalty by giving greater pay, more vacation, health policies, and retirement pensions. Businesses did not have a profit margin but a "giving" margin. They literally wanted to give you more value for your money.

For instance, since gas prices are what they are, in 1959 gas was $0.32/gallon in Riverton, Wyoming, according to my dad. However, an 18-year-old today would not know that you could buy Premium Regular gas at the pump, which had an octane rating of 99! No wonder they liked to drag race the cars on the street! "Premium" gas today in the U. S. is rated at 91 octane. Not only was the gas a better quality for the price, you had everything checked on your car along with having your windows washed. This was not full-service, this was "normal" service at a gas station.

This time was not only a golden age, but is an era that remains timeless in some cases because of what came out of it, besides Elvis, Johnny Cash, and Marilyn Monroe. Many aspects of our culture came out of this time period. As my dad said, "There was a lot of what was and a lot of what wasn't."

"A LOT OF WHAT WAS"

Unless you were also from this generation, many of us do not know what we missed in the Fifties, some of this being very good and some of this detrimental, depending on our perspective. The "nuclear" family was the norm for this time period, which referred to one mom, one dad, and the children from their marriage. Families ate together, shared the chores, contributed to the whole family financially, and took vacations or saw other family members as a unit. My dad started work at J.C. Penney when he was sixteen at $0.60/hr. This was a big name in Wyoming, since Mr. Penney started out in Kemmerer. This paycheck was not just his, but he paid for his fair share along with supporting his parents. A gender gap did not quite exist, because the family was integral to everything.

Morality was not a concept, but was understood as "the way to be" during the Fifties. Almost everyone in my dad's neighborhood kept the doors to their homes and cars unlocked. Divorce was extremely rare. Teen pregnancy was not even in the dictionary. If two people discussed business and made a deal, their word or their handshake was their bond, even contract in many cases. Businesses did not need the legal paperwork to make something "legal." People paid their taxes and felt shame if they owed somebody money or a favor.

Respect resided at every level of society. Children respected their parents, their teachers, or anyone in authority. My dad said, "Children did not usually speak unless they were spoken to." My dad had one exception when he had his paper route as a kid. Even then, he learned from Jerry Spence, who was in his paper route, "It is not 'Can I collect, but may I collect?'" Teachers were respected. Government officials were respected at every level. The Media was respected as a trustworthy, unbiased news source. The military was clearly portrayed as honorable. This included President Eisenhower along with most WWII veterans alive displaying respect, integrity, honor, and duty.

Delayed gratification was a common practice in every facet of life. People waited until marriage to experience sexual intimacy, and in many cases, this even included kissing! People knew they had to earn something before they could receive it. Children had to earn the next grade level by passing their final exam. Credit was not the norm. People would earn the money first in order to buy something or view the product desired. For example, a goal was a down payment of $5,000 for a new home. Remember, a new home came with an average cost of $30,000, so people were literally waiting until they had 20-25% to put down on the loan. Many cars were still paid for in cash, like my dad did with his first car, a 1950 Plymouth, Special Deluxe convertible.

Money, in quality and concept, was handled differently. "A penny saved was a penny earned." Other than the penny, every other coin was made of silver, so no one threw change away. Most Americans saved 10-25% of their income and gave at least 10% to charity because most people in this time frame were taught to tithe to their local church or synagogue. Therefore, most Americans lived on around 75% of their income in a year. Money was seen as an exchange for goods or services rendered. Money was a means of getting things needed for living or doing business, not as a huge status symbol.

MONEY WAS A MEANS OF GETTING THINGS NEEDED, NOT AS A HUGE STATUS SYMBOL

Bikinis were actually created in the 1950's, something my dad as a man and a J.C. Penney employee, could remember. Now just think of this one creation. This was a culture shock to say the least! This is a time when the poodle skirts were fashionable and down to the ankles. Along with this, a guy by the name of Hugh Hefner came out with a magazine entitled *Playboy*. We could say the rest of this is history!

The beginning of the Cold War and fast food marked this period. If this were in the Greek verb tense, I would say it were in the perfect tense, because it started, but continues to have results in our present time. The Cold War sparked a military buildup along with shelter placements in every local community. In my part of the world, we still have the "missile fields" all around. The Russians launched the first satellite in 1957, so a huge face-off had begun with weaponry and ingenuity.

The fast food franchises had some pep in getting started with drive-ins such as A&W® and Tastee-Freez® because they became the places to hang out for the "cruisers." Money may not have been much of a status symbol, but the car that a guy owned was a representation of who he was. I mentioned my dad's car, but he had friends with cars like a '53 MG, '55 Ford, or '58 Chevy Impala. Along with the cruisers, there were certain goals attained in Riverton, Wyoming. The class of '59 would try to make it from Shoshoni to Casper in an hour! This was not our modern highway, but a narrow, two-lane, 100 mile road that went through various small towns en route. Risk taking was big then, not just in school pranks or dares on the highway, but in business and life in general.

"A LOT OF WHAT WASN'T"

What if time stood still at this point? What is the point where you wanted it to stand still?

Worry or fear was not common, especially for the future in reference to what we would do or how we would live. However, what would have been missed if time was inevitably stuck? My dad shared a number of things that may have been thought of, but were not in everyday life.

Let us consider fuel injection. This was actually invented during the fifties and could be found on something like a '57 Corvette, but did not fully replace the carburetor until the

1990's. The fuel injector is much more efficient and can also deliver much more power. Now most of us younger Americans would not know what three two-barrel carburetors on a V-8 engine sounded like in a '58 Chevy Impala, so we may have missed out on some raw power. With the price of gas today, the carburetor may be frowned upon.

One other feature did not exist in cars, the child safety seat. I know this because three of us boys were just piled in the back of the car wherever we went, and I was not born in the fifties. When a mom had her baby, she would get seated in the front seat and then handed her newborn baby by the nurse. After that, the family would drive home.

Along with the big cars and the big engines, most of the country had narrow highways not made for speed or safety. President Eisenhower came up with the idea for the Interstate Highway System, but my dad said the system was not fully in place until after 1963. If we did not have this highway system, picture what driving would be like on a bunch of two lane roads, especially in high-traffic areas! Today, we can cruise safely across Wyoming in either direction at 75 mph and make a drive in half the time it would have taken someone over fifty years ago.

Now my ears picked up when my dad mentioned a particular beverage, beer. In Wyoming, there were four kinds of beer available: Hamm's, Miller, Coors, and Budweiser. That was it! Take note of the variations that existed for these kinds of beers. None! There were no wine coolers, light beers, and no pop top cans yet! My dad remembers when Coors was allowed to come into Wyoming, and that was a big deal! I attended the University of Wyoming. Even with the huge rivalry between our school and Colorado State University, we certainly enjoyed Odell's Brewing Company and New Belgium Brewing Company. So in the realm of beer, there was "a lot of what was not." For many of us, this would have been a huge loss if time stood still.

Now if beer is something that guys could relate to, shopping malls should appeal to the ladies. Shopping malls developed after the interstate highway system. They were nonexistent, except maybe in a few metropolitan areas. Most rural areas had everything to offer for the average American home in 1959. There was neither the need to drive, nor the desire to drive fifty miles just to get a pair of shoes. As a J.C. Penney employee, my dad noticed this trend. The shopping malls made a significant impact on how people spent their time and money. In places where winter was long, cold and windy, a warm place that was easy to access and walk in made for a good recreation area, not just shopping area.

When it came to shopping, portable electronics were non-existent, even the transistor radio had not been in mass production yet. The only "portable" radio most people had was their car radio. Cell phones, laptop computers, notebooks, and countless other portable electronic devices were being conceived and perceived as science fiction then.

Most people had no idea about drugs or drug use as something to consider in 1959. My dad did not know what they were until he and his friends went to a movie that portrayed someone with a drug addiction. Pharmaceutical drugs were also extremely limited. Aspirin was the only common pain reliever and was certainly not something to be addicted to. Recreational drug use was simply not in the vocabulary or the culture of this time.

RECREATIONAL DRUG USE WAS SIMPLY NOT IN THE VOCABULARY OR THE CULTURE OF THIS TIME

Civil Rights had certainly been sparked in the 1950's, but was not yet achieved in 1959. Rosa Parks boldly remained in her seat on the bus, December 1, 1955. However, the unity and focus of the Civil Rights movement reached the tipping point with Dr. Martin Luther King, Jr's "I Have a Dream" speech on August 28, 1963. What if time froze and this speech did not take place? I believe this was the most powerful prophetic proclamation of the 20th Century. The world, not just the United States, would be in a diminished place.

Women in the workplace had received a foothold thanks to WWII, with so many of the men off to war or occupation. Women as housewives or homemakers were the norm, but women had broken through glass ceilings within business, government, and the military. They had broken through, but their numbers were small. Other mountains still needed to be climbed such as the media, which remained predominantly male for a few more decades. The pay scale was off balance between men and women, with men receiving more in many professions in 1959.

Nursing homes or hospices were few in number, because families cared for their own family members. Grandparents, and most other relatives, lived within the same community, so support systems existed in numbers, making the responsibility of care part of the family duty. In this regard, extended families were not fragmented since most of them could find work or take over the family business within their home town.

I did mention that *Playboy* began in 1953, but there was not any kind of pornography on the scale that exists today. Popular TV shows with married couples had twin beds in the bedroom because the thought of what happened in the bedroom was left as a mystery for a vast majority of people until marriage. The digital age was decades away, and the information age of delivering videos through mass marketing was the same. As mentioned earlier, dealing with the family, divorce was pretty rare in these days. Could there be a correlation between the two?

There was no such thing as the Internet. Phones had a chord attached to them, and most people did not have a push-button phone. If you know what a rotary phone is, it gives your age away! If you do not know what a rotary phone is, ask your parents or even grandparents what that was. There were no computers to type term papers. They were completed using a good old-fashioned typewriter!

WHAT IF WE WERE STUCK HERE?

We could go on with a list one mile long on both sides of the column of what was and what wasn't in 1959. Depending on our perspective, we may be joyful that many of these things mentioned are in place today. In this list, we may want to abandon, even outlaw some things on the list. I was overjoyed when one place made a "No emails on Friday" policy, so we could actually get our real work accomplished and have a relaxing weekend. If you could make two columns, what aspects or qualities would you want to keep and which ones would you want to eliminate? Now consider your own life. Going back to the beginning, what is the ditch you are stuck in?

We may be thinking that it is impossible to be stuck in time, because time keeps on ticking. For the record, my father is not stuck in time, because he even has a Facebook account. I did choose the year 1959 as a reference point, not just because my dad graduated from high school that year. This was a pivotal year in our nation's history for what happened beforehand as well as what happened afterward.

In the depth of our souls, minds, and emotions, we can be stuck in a certain place, a pivotal place, specifically where that area of greatest loss happened. The sticking point may also be where we experienced some form of trauma, from combat to an accident. Unless we do some honest reasoning, we could be stuck in that chronological place forever, even though time keeps on ticking.

Oftentimes, we do not get out of the ditch on our own. As I have shared some of my personal journey, I had to have some assistance along this path we call life. My hope is all of us can relate to needing assistance as well as receiving the assistance being offered. I am writing this, knowing I have been in a place to enable others to achieve forward momentum and gain some solid traction. Hopefully, we are gaining revelation and self-awareness to not only get us moving, but also assist the people we love and care for in our families, communities, businesses, religious assemblies, cities, and even our nation.

WHAT IS THE AMERICAN DREAM?

This is a question worth asking repeatedly. What is the American dream? We may need to do a little treasure hunting to discover this one. For the Founding Fathers, the American dream was a matter of principle, faith, freedom, equality, a voice in the public and political arena and opportunity. The Founding Fathers actually narrowed it down to the "inalienable rights of life, liberty, and the pursuit of happiness."[3]

For my maternal and paternal ancestors, the American dream meant new beginnings, a new way of life, freedom, and opportunity. I want to have what the Founding Fathers fought for and what my ancestors lived out. I mentioned my dad's parents, now consider my mom's parents. They worked 1000 acres in North Dakota with all of their might, creativity, and perseverance. They planted crops and raised cattle, pigs, and poultry, along with seven children. My grandmother did not go to a doctor until after her fourth child! By their own sweat equity, they paid for all of that land and passed on that same tenacity to their children's children, and I am one of them. I do not want security for my family, I want freedom. I do not want my family to be a burden to society, I want all of us to be contributors. I want my daughters and my son to have the same opportunities and share the same values I have. I want them to be leaders and influencers in whatever field they choose.

Now let us personalize this. How would you define *your* American dream? How would you define this dream for your family? How would you define this dream for your community? How would you define this dream for your business? Now how would you define this dream for the nation and how would your dream influence this nation?

In defining the American dream for ourselves and our families, perhaps we can identify what we have lost versus what we have gained. Historically this is nothing new, but has been an issue throughout history. Let us pursue this in a context outside of our own.

POINTS TO PONDER

1. What is the Golden Age for you?

2. What is the ditch or event that you are stuck in?

3. In order to define the sticking point in time, make two columns and label them "What was" and "What wasn't." Then fill these in with as many qualities or aspects you remember.

4. Which qualities would you want to keep and which ones would you want to eliminate?

5. How would you define your American dream? Depending on where you are in life and who you influence, make a personal page, family page, community page, business page and national page.

6. How would you be able to fulfill your American dream?

7. How would your dream influence the nation?

Endnotes

1. Personal interview with Jack Jensen, March 28, 2013.
2. Personal interview with Jack Jensen, March 28, 2013.
3. *The Declaration of Independence,* July 4, 1776.

CHAPTER 6

ROME, 409 A.D.

Those who do not learn from history are doomed to repeat it.
—Edmund Burke

The United States was not the first republic to have a dream. Rome started out as a city-state, then became a republic, and finally transitioned to an empire when Caesar claimed ultimate authority as a "god."[1] The Roman republic had achieved a certain level within civilization and the known world of the time as the most advanced, most powerful, and most thriving culture. The Roman influence was so great that many people wanted to buy their citizenship if they were not born a citizen.[2]

The reason for this chapter title is to emphasize the time period before Rome was sacked by Alaric and the Visigoths on August 20, 410 AD.[3] This is the year before all previous assumptions would be shattered, when the watchmen were on the walls for prestige rather than necessity. We can question what led to the demise of such a great civilization. Different scholars and historians since the Roman collapse have argued what was the actual cause of the empire crumbling.[4] On that basis, I offer some other hypotheses, which contributed to the fall of such a great civilization: pathological grief along with the "Hezekiah Complex," which I will define later. I believe the Roman citizens heard so much about the *"pax romana,"* or "Roman peace," they longed for this decades or centuries past its climax, or even perceived climax. The *pax romana* referred to the Roman Empire at its greatest level in conquest and culture around the 1st century. The social elite would focus on what they had lost along with focusing on themselves so much, they probably lost sight of the fact their civilization could be destroyed. Eventually, the city that represented everything about their society and culture was sacked.

I believe Constantine had an intuition nearly a century earlier when he moved his throne and central power to Constantinople. He saw the citizens as well as the social elite unwilling to give up the past and move toward a different, perhaps even a brighter future. They were "stuck in the mud" of pathological grief. The people who shared Constantine's perception are the ones who helped establish Constantinople and the Eastern Empire for centuries following the fall of Rome. Amazingly, this "Eastern Empire" continued in one form or another until the year Constantinople was sacked in 1453 AD. Due to moving out of the pathological grief of the previous Roman Empire, this civilization continued for over one thousand years after the siege of Rome.

"PAX ROMANA"
VS. "PAX AMERICANA"[5]

What did the Roman Empire have during the period known as *pax romana*? The first aspect is a written language and very accurate record keeping. We do not have to delve deep at all to realize they wanted people to be able to carry on Roman business, government, religion, architecture, art, education and entertainment.

In all civilizations, expansion comes along with the commerce. The original Roman colonies expanded with their neighbors in order to have better trade, better crops, and a better quality of life. At the height of the Roman Empire, "all roads did lead to Rome" because the demand for the best products the world had to offer was the greatest at the epicenter. As the empire expanded, trade routes were acquired. The examples of masonry, metallurgy, mosaics, shipbuilding, pottery, and weaponry from this time period clearly indicate expert craftsmanship. Since many of these examples exist outside of the empire, their economy had to be the largest in the world at the time.

Even after the fall of the Roman republic, the names of government officials and government terms are still used from the original Latin terms that gave them definition. Augustus divided the empire into eleven regions.[6] This was for financial as well as political reasons.[7] This way each person could vote in his place of origin.[8] They had a representative form of government established. They even had an organized postal service.[9] However, they also had ways of keeping people in line. Besides the most advanced military in the known world, the "cat o' nine tails" and the "cross" were two gruesome instruments of punishment. Roman citizens were spared torture in the form of the crucifix, which was meant for foreigners or criminals.

The Roman religion started out as its own, but the Hellenistic influence along with other cultures made room for all kinds of worship in the Roman world. Some of the most ornate and colossal buildings were the temples dedicated to different deities, depending on the area and depending on the influence. In the first century, the Temple of Artemis (Diana) in Ephesus was considered one of the great wonders of the world because of its size. For the most part, the Roman Empire was surprisingly tolerant of other religions. No doubt, religion played a huge role in the culture.

When it came to Roman architecture, not just the temples were magnificent. Everything was magnificent! Who does not want to go to Rome today to see the historical landmarks which still stand, such as the Colosseum? My grandma remembers when indoor plumbing showed up, but the Romans had that two thousand years ago! Many aqueducts still stand today as a testimony to their advancement. The Roman arch used in construction has allowed them to stand for millennia. Their arch system for bridges are still seen and observed across Europe because some of these bridges are still in use. The Roman version of cement still has been unmatched. Their use of geometry was astounding, which can still be observed in the Parthenon today, with a perfect sphere shape in its dome.

The Roman method of building roads is the same method we use today in the United States. The Roman road system was unmatched compared to any other civilization.

Art was apparent in everything as well. From statues, to military armor, to the architecture, the craftsmanship these people wielded was astounding. For some reason, warfare ignites ingenuity and creativity. Even though other cultures learned how to forge iron, the Romans possessed ornate armor, projectiles, the signature Roman shield, double-edged swords, and the strategy to combine all of their forces into unstoppable siege warfare. The mosaics captured the life and culture of the Roman civilization, from rituals to everyday chores such as bathing or picking crops. The same can be said for the stonecutting or pottery, which would also capture those lively moments as if they were actually frozen in time.

With all the advancements the Romans achieved, they needed to pass their expertise on to the next generation. Education did exist, but became more developed as the empire endured. Thanks to assimilation, Greek literature and philosophy permeated the known world. Greek was still one of the universal languages of the time. Many cities were known as places of learning besides Rome. Carthage, Alexandria, Antioch, Tarsus, and Athens are just a few cities known for their education. Depending on one's family line or position, a better education could be acquired.

The entertainment industry has existed since the dawn of civilization, but some took it to a whole new level. In nearly every Roman city, an amphitheater was built. The Roman

Colosseum still stands, as mentioned, but other cities held the gladiator games along with other events. The gladiator games made sport of people, usually slaves killing each other, or gladiators fighting wild animals or reenacting ancient battles. Anyone would have been impressed with the chariot race track, the Circus Maximus, even by today's standards! This was the NASCAR of the first century, and was believed to be capable of holding up to 150,000 spectators.

When it comes to all of the different spheres of Roman culture and their prestige in their glory days, could you picture these juxtaposed to those of the United States? When it comes to business, we still have the greatest economy in the world, at least for now. Our form of government has become known as the "Great Experiment." Will it continue to function, or will the experiment end like a chemistry experiment gone wrong? In the area of religion, religion is tolerated so long as it does not interfere with public life or public policies. The United States has allowed the greatest religious freedom of any civilization. American influence in the form of art, architecture, and entertainment, has circumnavigated the globe. Some of this is coming to close proximity of what Rome had to offer.

The Roman Empire possessed the greatest centers of learning including Alexandria, Jerusalem, Syrian Antioch, Tarsus, and Rome. When it comes to higher education, many people in the world desire to attend an American university. So are we set to lose everything or are we yet to see our nation's brightest future? What is the script we are creating for our personal future?

OUR PERSONAL "PAX"

When it comes to our personal lives, what is the personal *"pax"* (peace) we want to attain? Are we trying to maintain a certain lifestyle? Perhaps the lifestyle we are maintaining may be mediocre to the one in our future, but we do not realize it. Now I am not painting a picture where we all drive a Bentley and live in a 10,000 square foot home. Some of the most joy-filled people in the world lead a very simplified life. However, if we are still stuck in that moment of time, believing that was our best time to live, then we have ceased living. We will only continue to look back and meditate on how great it was "back then." I want us all to grasp on to a future that is brilliant and joyful and pull it into the present.

So can we be honest and truly evaluate our current situations? Have we achieved the personal goals we had when we were kids? Have we poured our hearts and minds out to our family so a legacy can be carried on? Have we made a difference in our community? Are we serving the city or state we are residing in? Do we want to see our nation have a positive impact in this global arena?

WHAT FOUNDATION DO WE HAVE?

When it comes to our foundation, we must have this right and have it firm, or anything built on it is in vain and will never last. As I stated previously, from my own family heritage as well as being a citizen of the United States of America, freedom and opportunity are a part of this foundation. As I quoted before, "life, liberty, and the pursuit of happiness" was forged in the original design as part of our "unalienable rights."[10]

What other aspects have we added to our foundation? For my family, I want everyone to have the opportunity for higher education. We want to be contributors to society, not takers. We want to be free to choose the kind of living we would desire, whether in business, government, education, the media, arts and entertainment, or a religious profession.

If you come from a family successful in business, your foundation may include the opportunity to get started in the same line of business. Or if you are a doctor, perhaps you would like to see your son or daughter join you in keeping the family practice along with the same alma mater. Among my relatives in North Dakota, some are fourth and fifth generation farmers and ranchers.

Some communities or cities have certain occupations at their foundation. Hollywood goes without saying. Nashville has a reputation as well. So does Washington, D.C. After working in the medical arena, Cleveland has the word "Clinic" after it in my mind. They have a reputation for advanced medicine along with Mayo Clinic in Rochester, Minnesota. We could go through the country and label every city. My point is you know your community and your city better than anyone else and what lies at its core or foundation. Now if there has been a major loss such as a factory, business, or school, then you must grieve what has happened and pursue a new expectation.

SAINT AUGUSTINE SAW IT

I am not the first person to discuss grief on a national scale. However, Saint Augustine dealt with the grief of the people *after* their nation and civilization was defeated as well as diminished in his great work, *The City of God*. My hope is we can deal with the issues of our time before it is too late. I do not want to see our personal lives, families, communities, businesses and nation become shattered along with our assumptions. Wisdom can be learning from someone else's experience so we do not have to repeat the same thing. As my dad was a witness for 1959, Augustine can be our witness for 409 A.D. and the aftermath that followed.

Within a short period of time, Augustine lost his mother, Monica, his son, Adeodatus, and a close friend, Nebridius.[11] Based on the immense personal loss he experienced, Augustine could recognize an entire civilization grieving. So to save you from reading hundreds of pages, unless you want to, let me summarize his main thesis.

Christians within the Roman Empire thought this was part of the Kingdom of God. Augustine dealt with their loss along with their shattered assumptions. Rome was not the Kingdom of God and was merely a natural empire with a finite end. Even though they were in fact part of the Kingdom of God as individuals according to their theology, the kingdoms of this world are not a part of the Kingdom of God unless the citizens of any civilization within it chose to be. His main point was for the people of God he was addressing to go on living their lives to the fullest, being present, not just for themselves, but for their loved ones and for their neighbors. They were also advised to contemplate on God, who could not only change their hearts, but the times and seasons so that they would be even brighter and better than they could possibly imagine. He wanted them to see the possibility of a "city whose builder and maker was God."[12]

THE HEZEKIAH COMPLEX

In order to define the "Hezekiah Complex," I must first present some historical background and context. Hezekiah was king over the southern kingdom of Judah in Jerusalem when the Assyrians came to lay siege to the city.[13] He was gravely concerned for his own kingdom because the northern kingdom of Israel had already been conquered with the northern capital of Samaria having been sacked. Hezekiah obviously did not want to lose his kingdom, but was obviously concerned because his advisors met with him while he is calculating how much food and water the city would have to withstand a siege.[14] The king of Assyria sent a messenger to King Hezekiah and told him that he could not trust in his own strength or Egypt as an ally to defeat him. The messenger carried on and said he could not trust in anything including his God.

The Israelites had torn their clothes and put on sackcloth, which was their way of humbling themselves before God as a symbolic act indicating that only God could change their circumstances. This becomes the turning point for the Israelites because they go into mourning, perceiving and grieving their loss along with crying out to God for deliverance. Isaiah the

Prophet brought the message for them not to be afraid because God heard the blasphemies of the Assyrians and would deliver them. An angel of the LORD came into the camp and killed 185,000 of their soldiers.[15]

Just as the Israelites experienced a supernatural deliverance, Hezekiah became sick to the point of death immediately thereafter.[16] Once again, Hezekiah cried out to the LORD, thinking his days were few in number. His personal grief and petition to the LORD must have been genuine. Isaiah comes back to Hezekiah and proclaims he will not only live, but have fifteen years added to his life.[17] Hezekiah would not only live, but God would also give him a sign by moving the sun backward on the dial ten degrees.[18] So here is a man who went through intense grief due to a national crisis in the form of a siege on the land and city followed by a personal sickness that brought him to the point of death.

Now grief can affect us in peculiar ways, especially if we are elated that our circumstances came out the exact opposite of our expectations. Has this ever happened to you? Hezekiah was sent a gift from the king of Babylon through his envoys and Hezekiah proceeded to show them all of his wealth and his armory, literally showing them everything in his dominion.[19]

Then Isaiah declared to King Hezekiah everything he showed the envoys along with some of his own sons would be carried off to Babylon.[20] Instead of mourning, humbling himself, or crying out to the LORD, as he did in the previous situations, Hezekiah responded, "The word of the LORD which you have spoken is good! At least there will be peace and truth in my days."[21]

Now here in this response is the Hezekiah complex. First, Hezekiah did not go into mourning or cry out to the LORD to see if God would see a humble man and turn these circumstances around. Second, Hezekiah only thought of himself and the peace he would experience in his lifetime. He did not consider what the generation or generations would suffer based on his decisions. This included Hezekiah's own children! Yet, he did not have a change of heart. Of course, we know the rest is history. Babylon did lay siege to Jerusalem and took everything in 586 B.C.

There are numerous examples in history where this has been the case, but Hezekiah's are so detailed and descriptive. There

THE FATHERS HAVE EATEN SOUR GRAPES AND THE CHILDREN'S TEETH ARE SET ON EDGE

was another saying that summed up the Hezekiah Complex: "The fathers have eaten sour grapes and the children's teeth are set on edge."[22] This was proclaimed by the Israelites after the Babylonians had carried them off into captivity. Therefore, we do not want to make decisions that will affect or embitter the next generation. We want to make decisions that give the best future and best hope possible, for ourselves and the people we adore.

POINTS TO PONDER

1. What can we learn from our own past or your family's ancestry?

2. Are we set to lose everything or are we yet to see our nation's brightest future along with that of our own?

3. When it comes to our personal lives, what is the personal *"pax"* (peace) we want to attain or maintain?

4. So can we be honest and truly evaluate our current situations?

5. Are we thinking of the future generations and not just ourselves?

Endnotes

1. John 19:15, NKJV.

2. Acts 22:27-28, NKJV.

3. Ibid, p. 483.

4. Heather, Peter, *The Fall of the Roman Empire: A New History of Rome and the Barbarians* (Oxford University Press, New York, NY, 2006), p. xii.

5. Griffin, David Ray, and Scott, Peter Dale, editors, *9/11 and American Empire: Intellectuals Speak Out, Vol. 1* (Northampton, Mass: Olive Branch Press, 2007), p. 149-167.

6. Le Glay, Marcel, Voisin, Jean-Louis, and Yann Le Bohec, editors, with new material by David Cherry, Donald G. Kyle, and Eleni Namolaraki, *A History of Rome, 4th Edition*, (West Sussex, United Kingdom: Wiley-Blackwell Publishing, 2009), p. 239.

7. Ibid.

8. Ibid.

9. Ibid.

10. *Declaration of Independence,* July 4, 1776.

11. Augustine of Hippo, *The City of God,* translated by Marcus Dods (Peabody, MA: Hendrickson Publishers, Inc., 2010), p. ix.

12. Hebrews 11:10, NKJV.

13. Isaiah 36-37, NKJV.

14. Isaiah 36:2, NKJV.

15. Isaiah 37:36, NKJV.

16. Isaiah 38:1, NKJV.

17. Isaiah 38:5, NKJV.

18. Isaiah 38:8, NKJV.

19. Isaiah 39:2-4, NKJV.

20. Isaiah 39:5-7, NKJV.

21. Isaiah 39:8, NKJV.

22. Ezekiel 18:2, NKJV.

CHAPTER 7

HOW LONG WILL YOU GRIEVE FOR SAUL?[1]

You might be wondering, "What kind of question is this?" If you could take this question and replace "Saul" with the person, thing, event, moment, business, disaster, trauma or whatever else this could represent, then that is the question you must ask. When you do ask, keep in mind how long it has been since your particular loss occurred. But first, let me give some more details to this story in relation to the question.

Up until the time of King Saul Israel did not have a king, but judges who would be raised up to make decisions for the people as well as execute justice when the need arose. Samuel had been the judge over Israel for decades and traveled around the nation. As Samuel grew older, he had set his sons in place to be judges over the people following him. However, Samuel's sons did not possess the same integrity their father displayed.[2] Samuel thought the people were rejecting what he had done for the nation. God responded to him, "Heed the voice of the people in all that they say to you; for they have not rejected you, but they have rejected Me, that I should not rein over them."[3] Thus two characters feel a loss over this choice. These two characters are God and Samuel. But there is still more to the story.

A man named Saul was chosen to become king, but he did not live up to the expectations of anyone. Since "Saul was taller than all the people from the shoulders upward," one would suspect he would be a great man as well as a great king just due to his size.[4] We do not get too far into the story before all assumptions became shattered. The first incident occurred a couple years into his reign.[5] King Saul assumed the role of a prophet and offered a sacrifice to God which was the job of Samuel. Samuel had been a judge over Israel, but he was also the chosen prophet of the LORD. As soon as Saul finished doing something he should not have done, Samuel showed up.[6] Samuel rebuked him and told King Saul what he lost: "For now the LORD would have established your kingdom over Israel forever. But now your kingdom shall not continue. The LORD has sought for Himself a man after His own heart, and the LORD has commanded him to be commander over His people, because you have not kept what the LORD commanded you."[7]

The final nail in the coffin for King Saul came a little later. We are not certain, but enough time elapsed so that he could establish his sovereignty over Israel.[8] Saul was given another command through Samuel to utterly destroy the Amalekites, not leaving anything.[9] "The best indicator for future behavior is past performance."[10] Saul could have proven to be an effective leader as well as an effective listener, but he assumed certain things and kept the

THE BEST INDICATOR FOR FUTURE BEHAVIOR IS PAST PERFORMANCE

king alive along with the best animals. At this point Samuel confronted King Saul and said, "I will not return with you, for you have rejected the word of the LORD, and the LORD has rejected you from being king over Israel.[11]

Instead of gloating over the failure of King Saul, Samuel grieved for him and the decisions he had made. Remember, Samuel's sons were rejected as judges, so he could have enjoyed the fact that King Saul had failed. I believe this demonstrated the integrity of Samuel. I hope this is something we can emulate and pass on for generations. Nobody wants to see a person fail and then rejoice in it. Whether the person who fails is a local official, pastor, rabbi, business leader, or national leader, we should be grieved because their failure affects so many more people. The amazing part about this story is God did grieve as well.[12] He grieved for the nation of Israel because of how this one man's decisions would impact all of them. If the LORD grieved, then He had to come to a place of acceptance. That was the whole point of God's question. Will you come to a place of acceptance?

YOU MEAN TO TELL ME GOD GRIEVES?

Yes, God grieves. Please do not just take my word for it. In addition to the example I just presented in detail, several other references exist within Scripture. We are even told not to grieve the Holy Spirit.[13] If we are told not to do this, then it must be possible for us to achieve it. Within the Judeo-Christian framework, the first time God grieved was shortly after humankind had fallen away from paradise by disobeying. God grieved the loss of a broken relationship with Him along with a world that would feel the results of that one decision. The world became so evil God was grieved in His heart.[14] This was the first time God was grieved, but it certainly was not the last time.

Ezekiel heard from God and his language takes the language to another level. He said that God was "crushed" by the adulterous hearts of His people.[15] Have you ever felt grief at such a level it felt like a tremendous weight crushing all of life out of you? God obviously could not have the life crushed out of Him because He cannot die. But then again, He made a choice to do exactly that by coming and feeling the pain as a man. Isaiah said He was literally wounded for our transgressions and bruised, or crushed, for our iniquities.[16] So God truly knows the power of grief just as we do.

Knowing the power of grief, God actually gave instructions for His people to follow. This may seem too easy. However, this is not easy, but intentional. We must make a conscientious decision first to choose life.[17] By choosing life, I mean we must choose to live in the present and be fully present and no longer dwell on the past. So let us look at another situation where God gives a prescribed time.

I HAVE HOW MUCH TIME?

The people of Israel had experienced the supernatural deliverance of God from the most powerful empire at the time, the Egyptians. The LORD sent Moses into Egypt and performed ten miraculous signs, also known as "the plagues," convincing Pharaoh to free the Israelites from their centuries of slavery. Pharaoh reluctantly released all of them after the death of his firstborn son, who died with the rest of the firstborn in all of Egypt as the final plague.

Shortly after releasing the Israelites, Pharaoh relentlessly pursued the people of God to the Red Sea, assuming they were trapped. However, Moses once again proved to the people God can deliver them from anything by having a path dried out through the very heart of the Red Sea. All of the Israelites were able to get across with the plunder the Egyptians willingly gave them as they departed.[18] Being filled with rage, Pharaoh wanted revenge, chasing the Israelites into the path through the Red Sea, which ended with the water returning to its place and destroying the entire Egyptian army.

From that moment, Moses led the Israelites by way of a pillar of cloud by day and a pillar of fire by night for forty years in the desert. The Israelites lived in tents and were literally fed by God's provision of manna (which means "What is it?" in Hebrew) and quail, due to the people complaining. However, they did not need to hunt, fish, or plant crops, or gather anything else except what was already provided.

A camping trip lasting forty years would give everyone an opportunity to know each other very well, maybe too well! Since Moses was the leader, everyone would have known who he was. He was the leader who delivered them, spoke to God for them, received the Ten Commandments for them, judged them, and led them to victory in the battles they did fight in the desert. So when this national leader passed away, it was not a small loss. The entire nation of Israel would have been weeping for this man they had observed their entire lives. So how long did they have to weep for their leader? They had thirty days![19] That was it, just thirty days.

In the very next book, God assured the new leader, Joshua, that Moses was dead. A new time had come and it was time to move forward to what was in store for the nation, a land flowing with milk and honey. God assured Joshua He would be with him just as He was with Moses, and "He would not leave him or forsake him."[20] I want to assure you. You are not going through this by yourself. Do you believe your best days are still ahead of you?

MEMORIALIZING VS. IDOLIZING

In the stories I have shared about, did you also notice what everyone did or did not do? No one made a statue of the person or idolized them in any way. If we idolize someone or something, we literally create an idol out of it, which is placing the person or object above us, or even above God. This becomes a dangerous slippery slope. Both Saul and Moses died as leaders of the people of Israel. Moses was not bronzed, or mummified, which the Israelites learned how to do being in Egypt for over four hundred years. He was simply buried, and the amazing part is, nobody knows where![21] In order for the people to move forward in life, they could not carry an anchor weighing them down and keeping them in the past.

King Saul did die on the battlefield. He was mortally wounded, but ended up falling on his own sword because his armor bearer did not want to kill his king. The Philistines did idolize King Saul because they beheaded his body and hung it from the city walls in order to keep the people of Israel stuck in that moment, stuck in bitter defeat.[22] Do you think we have an enemy who would want us to idolize something and keep us meditating on that loss? The inhabitants of Jabesh Gilead must have had the spiritual sense to know King Saul's body had to come down in order for the people to choose life and go forward. Once King Saul's body was recaptured, he was still buried as well as honored along with his sons, because the people fasted seven days.[23]

We can create a memorial to a person, like we have for Abraham Lincoln in Washington, D.C. This can be a way of showing respect to a person who was tragically lost like he was to an assassination. We remember him along with Washington on President's Day. However, the United States still went forward after grieving the loss. We can have a memorial for an event, like D-Day, June 6, 1944. The memorial at Normandy, France, is in honor to the thousands of men who sacrificed their lives on that day in order to gain a foothold and defeat Nazi Germany. This memorial gave veterans who survived a safe place to release their feelings, process their grief, connect with fellow comrades, and leave there with a new sense of acceptance and a greater sense of purpose. The Memorials at Oklahoma City or at Ground Zero are also healthy examples. These are places for us to come and grieve in a healthy way without getting stuck in the loss or in the moment.

Now can we think of a person or event that is idolized? I can think of two people that link back to my dad's timeframe of 1959. Elvis is still called the king of Rock and Roll, but still leaves numerous people without a sense of closure. The same could be said for Marilyn Monroe. These two people are worshiped, and I do mean worshiped within our culture. Both of these icons gave people something to dream of, but this could not be reality for most of us. Numerous models and actresses have portrayed an image similar to Marilyn Monroe, because she is idolized within our culture. If we come into somebody's home where a tragic loss has occurred, such as a loss of children, and their pictures are bigger and more numerous than everything else, then we may have a case of idolization.

I know this loss is tremendous, but this does not allow the friends or family, or community to move forward. If we would happen to notice something like this, we must first know the people and walk with them through it before we say anything. The most powerful thing I have been able to say before is nothing, simply sitting in somebody's living room and weeping with the family. We must lovingly help people forward, not push them through or push them away. We must learn the art of listening with a gift of compassion. In some cases a professional may need to coach them through the process.

THE MOST POWERFUL THING I HAVE BEEN ABLE TO SAY IS NOTHING

GRIEF DOES NOT FORGET!

I have been reminded of grief in my own life as well as walking through other people's lives with their experiences. Just recently, I was eating dinner and looked up to see a man who looked almost exactly like a friend of mine who had passed away due to cancer. He was even wearing a Hawaiian shirt like he did. Instantly tears welled up in my eyes and I found myself engulfed in a wave of grief. Even though I was not consciously thinking of my friend, the grief remembered my friend and the loss I had experienced.

We may mark the calendar thirty days from now and declare a time to move on, but grief does not forget. This is another reason that idolization can keep us captive. If you remember my model of how the grief process works, any object, person, or triggered memory can leave us in the middle of that process going back and forth like a pin-ball between the steps of grief not knowing where we will come out. Certain smells or sounds can take us right back to that moment of loss and we must be aware of it. In the case of many veterans, a sudden feeling of anger to the point of rage comes to the surface because the grief came to the surface from some sort of trigger. Dates and anniversaries of an event are a trigger. What do we do to get out of this rut?

This is getting to the heart of why I put this in writing. When closure eludes us and grief reminds us, what do we do? I would say this is the million dollar question people want answered. However, this is not like ordering a "Happy Meal" and then feeling happy a few minutes later. This will take some discipline, effort, intentionality, forgiveness, grace and compassion. Since you are reading this, you have realized this cannot be achieved on your own. So let's walk through this together.

POINTS TO PONDER

1. How long will you grieve for your loss?

2. Will you come to a place of acceptance?

3. Have you ever felt grief at such a level it felt like a tremendous weight crushing all of life out of you?

4. Do you believe your best days are still ahead of you?

5. Have you idolized someone or something from your past?

6. Grief does not forget, but how can you learn from that moment and move forward?

Endnotes

1. I Samuel 16:1, NKJV.
2. I Samuel 8:3, NKJV.
3. I Samuel 8:7, NKJV.
4. I Samuel 10:23, NKJV.
5. I Samuel 13:1, NKJV.
6. I Samuel 13:10, NKJV.
7. I Samuel 13:13-14, NKJV.
8. I Samuel 14:47, NKJV.

9.   I Samuel 15:3, NKJV.

10. A quote often used by Rev. W. Dean Dyk.

11. I Samuel 15:26, NKJV.

12. I Samuel 15:35, NKJV.

13. Isaiah 63:10; Ephesians 4:30, NKJV.

14. Genesis 6:6, NKJV.

15. Ezekiel 6:9., NKJV

16. Isaiah 53:5, NKJV.

17. Deuteronomy 30:19, NKJV.

18. Exodus 12:35-36, NKJV.

19. Deuteronomy 34:8, NKJV.

20. Joshua 1:5, NKJV.

21. Deuteronomy 34:6, NKJV.

22. See I Samuel 31, NKJV.

23. I Samuel 31:13, NKJV.

YOU CANNOT NOW
BELIEVE THAT YOU WILL
EVER FEEL BETTER. BUT
THIS IS NOT TRUE. YOU
ARE SURE TO BE HAPPY
AGAIN. KNOWING THIS,
TRULY BELIEVING IT
WILL MAKE YOU LESS
MISERABLE NOW. I
HAVE HAD ENOUGH
EXPERIENCE TO MAKE
THIS STATEMENT.

—ABRAHAM LINCOLN

CHAPTER 8

HOW DO WE OVERCOME WHEN CLOSURE ELUDES US?

Hope deferred makes the heart sick,
but a longing fulfilled is a tree of life.
—Proverbs 13:12

We can become deeply entrenched in the grieving process with closure nowhere in sight. Referring to the model for grief, picture yourself in the middle and see the diagram as a merry-go-round, only it is not very merry. We can keep spinning around, not knowing at what point we may be thrown off. We could land right back in anger or depression, or finally reach acceptance only to be sucked back into despair and depression.

Pick any number of personal or public examples where closure eludes—a missing person, an unresolved case, a business failure without explanation, etc. I have picked a story that you may be familiar with, but perhaps have not considered in the context of grief. I chose this story because the lessons provided are a springboard for us jumping out of our mire.

JOSEPH

Joseph had a normal life considering the time period and the lifestyle of nomadic people caring for livestock. Families were large and sons were needed to tend the sheep and look after the interests of the family business. Joseph's father, Jacob, had eleven sons with Joseph being the second youngest.

Joseph was favored by his father, which certainly colored the family dynamics. His dad even made him a special tunic of many colors distinguishing him from his brothers.[1] There were already issues of jealousy and Joseph strained the relationship further when he brought a bad report about them to Jacob.[2] He was a dreamer and his dreams were so vivid, he could not help but describe them in detail to his father and brothers. Since the dreams had themes of his family bowing down to him, one might guess this did not go over very well.[3]

On one occasion, Joseph was sent by his father to check on his brothers along with the flocks. As he was approaching, the boys conspired to kill him. The plot was stopped by his brother, Reuben, who interceded for Joseph and convinced the rest to have him thrown in a pit instead of killed. Reuben planned to return and rescue Joseph later, but that is not what happened. An opportunity arose when some Midianite traders came buy and the brothers seized the moment to rid themselves of Joseph and make a profit. They ended up selling him into slavery to the travelers who in turn took Joseph down to Egypt and sold him to Potiphar, Captain of Pharaoh's Guard. The brothers stripped off the colored tunic and dipped it in goat's blood and made up a story about a lion killing Joseph. They brought this report back to Jacob, which was so grievous to him he said he would go to his grave in mourning.[4]

Joseph served faithfully as Potiphar's slave, and Potiphar noticed he had an administrative skill and placed him over everything. Considering he was a slave, he seemed to thrive in his circumstance. He caught the notice of Potiphar's wife and she offered him her bed, but Joseph refused to insult his master or his God.[5] Potipher's wife was insulted by the rebuttal and one day when Joseph was caught alone in the house she grabbed him by his garment to seduce him. Joseph ran out leaving the cloak behind. She accused him of trying to rape her and said he ran away after she screamed. Obviously, Potiphar believed his wife, was angered at Joseph, and had him thrown in prison.[6] So how much lower could Joseph get than being labeled as a slave rapist? This was following his own brothers selling him as a slave!

HOW MUCH WORSE COULD THINGS GET?

Joseph was shown mercy by the LORD in the prison and also received favor from the prison keeper, who must have noticed his skills, or perhaps had seen a pattern from Potiphar's household. Either way, Joseph was placed in charge of everything in the prison.[7] Then a time came when Pharaoh's baker and cupbearer were thrown in prison. They each had a dream and Joseph gave an accurate interpretation which was proven when it came to pass.[8] The baker and cupbearer were both released and returned to Pharaoh's service.

Two years later, Pharaoh had dreams which disturbed him greatly, but no one could interpret them. The cupbearer remembered Joseph's ability, so mentioned him to Pharaoh.[9] Joseph was summoned from prison and brought to the throne. God gave him the interpretation to Pharaoh's dreams, that seven years of abundance would be followed by seven years of severe famine. Joseph also gave Pharaoh the solution of how the abundance must be managed in order to survive the seven years of famine. When he had given the interpretation and the solution, Pharaoh made him Prime Minister over the entire empire, saying only his throne was greater![10]

After all Joseph had been through, what if he would have been stuck in his grief? What if he had stayed angry, depressed, or apathetic and not moved forward to accepting his "new normal?" Do you believe he would have been offered the position as an administrator twice, only to one day be providentially placed in charge of an empire? We do know Joseph moved forward and the keys to freedom lie in the next few chapters of his amazing story.

FORGET ABOUT IT!

Pharaoh gave Joseph a wife and from this marriage he had two sons. Both of these sons symbolically represent what Joseph proactively did in his life to overcome his loss. He named the first son Manasseh, which literally means "making forgetful."[11] Joseph said, "For God has made me forget all my toil and all my father's house."[12] I want you to notice two points. First, "making forgetful" has some action behind it. This is intentional. This is choosing not to dwell on the events that transpired. Second, God was the one who made him forget! Do we want to go forward? Do we wish to excel in our future? Perhaps we need some kind of assistance to get out of the cycle of grief and forget about the situation. Whether this is God or an instrument of God in the form of a chaplain, pastor, rabbi, life coach, counselor or person we find trustworthy, let's be deliberate about forgetting the past and focusing forward.

BE FRUITFUL

Joseph had a second son and named him Ephraim, literally meaning "fruitfulness."[13] So we not only must forget, we must be proactive in being fruitful in our lives once again. Joseph was given a unique opportunity to become Prime Minister, but he was fruitful as a slave and he was fruitful in the prison. Joseph began to be fruitful from the time he was sold as a slave to Potiphar. He must have come to a place of acceptance, realizing the family he knew may never see his face again. We must make the conscientious choice to produce something following our past loss or wounds, in spite of them if we must. If we wait around until we have closure or things return to how we think they should be, then there will never be the "right" time. Now, in this present moment. Now is the acceptable time.[14] Wherever and whenever you are, be there!

WILL YOU RELEASE OTHERS?

Joseph found another key to be free of the past, but it was not an easy one. This is a simple concept, but difficult for many of us to practice. In the midst of the severe famine, ten of his brothers showed up to buy grain because they had run out of food in Canaan. Since they believed him a slave or dead and he had become fluent in the Egyptian language and was dressed as an Egyptian, his brothers did not recognize him. Joseph had the advantage when they appeared before him. He could have them killed or thrown out as Prime Minister, but he did not. Instead, he gave them the food they asked for and even gave them their money back.

Joseph wanted to see his youngest brother, Benjamin, who had not made the journey. He bargained without revealing his identity, keeping one of the brothers in Egypt and promising no harm if they would return with their youngest brother. This caused great fear in Jacob. He was reluctant to allow Benjamin to make the journey, still wounded from the loss of Joseph, his favorite.

The brothers did eventually make the long journey and return to Egypt with Benjamin. When Joseph saw all of them together, he was flooded with grief and joy simultaneously. He had to leave their presence at first so they would not see the second mightiest man in Egypt as a weakling. He invited all of them to a meal and made sure all were seated in birth order, from the oldest to the youngest. Joseph's brothers started to realize something was going on, and then Joseph revealed himself to them. What would his brothers have thought at this point?

I believe some were in fear for their lives, but Joseph forgave them for what they did, saying, "But now, do not therefore be grieved or angry with yourselves because you sold me here; for God sent me before you to preserve life."[15] He had moved on from the past and literally saw their actions as the hand of God placing him so that he could preserve their lives in the future. Joseph saw his adversity through the filter of God's purpose.

JOSEPH SAW HIS ADVERSITY THROUGH THE FILTER OF GOD'S PURPOSE

THERE IS PURPOSE IN PAIN

As a chaplain, one of the hardest situations is being there for parents who have lost a child. I cannot help weeping with those who weep. I have been in an emergency room when a father was given the notification his nine year old son could not be resuscitated after drowning in a hot tub. I have been the one who has gone into a family's home with a commanding officer to notify the parents their 20 year old Marine had been killed in action in Iraq. These are extremely difficult circumstances, but when there is a situation involving murder, something more is added to it. Now there is an offender to receive the deluge of anger, there is someone to blame all our grief upon.

Andy and Kate Grosmaire had a daughter, Ann, who was murdered by her 19-year-old boyfriend, Conor McBride, with his dad's shotgun.[16] Many of us would hope for the maximum penalty, but that is not what the Grosmaires, pursued. They actually asked for him to receive a fifteen year sentence.[17] As surprising as this was, they did not stop there.

Andy and Kate made the proactive choice to forgive Conor. Andy said, "We are not offering a pardon to him. Forgiveness frees us. It keeps us from going to prison with Conor."[18] They continue to go and visit him once a month in prison.[19] Conor received a sentence for twenty years in prison, but now it includes the forgiveness of Ann's parents and a twenty year sentence of compassion on the part of Andy and Kate. Perhaps we could follow their example to release others like this.

WILL YOU FORGIVE YOURSELF?

Sometimes, the very person we must forgive is ourselves.[20] We may limit ourselves through shame or guilt, but we can break free from this cycle. Many times our worst enemy is us. Our "self-talk" can be enough to keep us condemned and walking with our heads down. Have you ever stopped to listen to what your mind is saying? If your own talk is negative, perhaps it is time to get a different program or track playing. Once again, this will take some focus and willingness to change the recording, just as it would be to change the music or station within your living room. However, our mind is not instantaneous like a TV with a remote control, or a smart phone receiving a new "app." We must create a new pathway in our brain. This may take the help of a professional and it may take more than thirty days, but it is achievable. To receive a better outcome, we must understand that the effort and discomfort involved is worth it.

FINDING PURPOSE

Joseph mentioned he was brought to Egypt to "preserve life." He had a purpose statement 3900 years before it was popular! People can develop the will to survive if they have a compelling enough reason. Viktor Frankl's classic work, *Man's Search for Meaning,* is a great resource to understand the value of purpose.[21] As a psychologist and a prisoner in a Nazi death camp, Viktor witnessed the power of purpose sustain his life along with many others. Under the circumstances he described, it would be pretty easy to give up. No matter what happened, Viktor envisioned himself teaching in Austria, and that is exactly what he did following his freedom after the end of the war. What is the purpose you envision for yourself? If you are unsure what your purpose might be, ask those within your inner circle what gifts and talents they see in your possession.

THE POWER OF PROCLAMATION

Going back into Joseph's story, we can see how he used proclamation in his present circumstances to pull the future he desired toward him. When Joseph declared the two dreams given to Pharaoh by God would come to pass, he was not saying that just for Pharaoh's benefit. Joseph made a proclamation on his behalf as well. Recall that he received two dreams in which he saw his brothers bowing down to him.[22] Pharaoh did not know of Joseph's dreams, but Joseph remembered his own dreams. When he spoke in faith to Pharaoh, he was declaring his own dreams would come to pass. They surely did!

Following the economic crisis on September 15, 2008, the Ford Motor Company was one of the corporations declaring it would not take any bailout money. They were in a position where they did not owe anything and could focus on the future without any hooks from the past. They have since launched to be the top ranked seller of cars and trucks in the world. Obviously, just as Joseph was in place to get Egypt and the known world out of a seven year famine, some key leaders at Ford were in place to make the right decisions at the opportune time to make the company excel.

Taking this to a national context, Guatemala was crippled with a stagnant economy. They were in a position where they imported many more products than they could export, and this was further complicated by greed and corruption. Numerous people within the nation became fed up with the circumstances which seemed impossible to overcome. But they prayed for the impossible to happen and declared it would happen. They declared Guatemala would export more than it imported. Can you guess what happened? Do you know which nation many businesses moved into with manufacturing plants? Surely, Guatemala now exports much more than they import and has an economy experiencing an exponential growth rate.

THEY PRAYED FOR THE IMPOSSIBLE TO HAPPEN AND DECLARED IT WOULD HAPPEN

This may not have happened overnight, but it did happen! One area around Almolonga experienced a 1000% increase in its crop production because of a dramatic breakthrough, which you can see for yourself in George Otis Jr.'s documentary.[23]

A CLOSING CEREMONY

Sometimes, we must take matters into our own hands. We must make a daring decision to say, "Enough is enough!" When we do experience loss on a grand scale, we must have courage. Courage can simply mean that even when we do not want to move forward, we do anyway. I believe the city of New Orleans had some perceptive leaders who realized their city needed some kind of focal point for closure.

At the five year anniversary of Hurricane Katrina, religious leaders led their city through ceremonies to mark a time of closure to the loss and a time to start living once again. On August 28, 2010, the Catholic Church held a mass and funeral for the city. On the following day, an Interfaith ceremony was held to assist people of the city have a final opportunity to grieve their losses and bury the event.

One great example of this movement on the five year anniversary was a casket used to hold notes, trinkets, or pieces of the devastation followed by the lid being slammed shut. Then it was taken to a cemetery and buried to signify enough time had passed and that people have now shut the door on the pain and memories. Burying the reminders was symbolic—they can no longer be "dug up" in the future. Is this something any of us can use personally? Indeed. Could we perform this in a business? Absolutely! This was performed in a community and in a city, and it can be effective on any scale, no matter how great or small.

REBIRTH THE DATE
AS A CELEBRATION!

This may seem counterintuitive, especially after something tragic. I worked in a neurological institute and learned from the experts we can retrain the brain. We must be deliberate and religious about creating a new neural pathway that replaces an existing superhighway of pain and loss. One of my close friends, Ben, was born on September 11. Is he supposed to stop celebrating his birthday? In our culture, we celebrate birthdays no matter what age we turn. We may not always be honest about how old we are, but we will still celebrate the event! Ben still celebrates his birthday on September 11.

Could this be any different for us? Not really, this is just that simple. What if someone was held in the human trafficking and sex slave industry for years, but managed to break free? Unfortunately, for millions of people, this is a reality. Are they supposed to stop living? Absolutely not, but on the contrary, they have a reason to celebrate life and enjoy a new future filled with hope. What if they took their day of freedom and turned that day into a day of celebration, like a liberty birthday?

We do this for the nation on July 4, Independence Day. Why not do this for ourselves and celebrate our personal independence? In Celebrate Recovery or Alcoholics Anonymous, the individuals celebrate their sobriety birthday within the group, because it is celebrating that time of new beginnings. This has worked for my dad since 1978, so it can work for you and me as well. Take those scars and turn them into stars, into fireworks, into something festive.

ALL OR NOTHING!

When I do something, I am an "all or nothing" kind of person. How about you? I believe this is the attitude we must take in order to get unstuck and moving forward again. Perhaps we only need to do a few of these steps and we will feel the shackles fall off our heart, soul and mind. Some of us may need to implement all of these steps and incorporate them as daily reminders for a year.

Independence is a badge of honor for Americans. There are few qualities that resonate so clearly and universally with us. We may be independently minded, but this should not hinder us from reaching out. We may need some guidance or affirmation to get through those spots lacking a concise closure. If shame, fear, or guilt still grips us, we must find the trustworthy professional or friend who can bring us to the light. Whatever it takes, you know yourself. But I say we all pick up New Hampshire's motto, "Live Free or Die." Living is a choice. "I have set before you life and death—choose life."[24]

QUESTIONS TO CONSIDER

1. Are you able to forget about a past event or great loss?

2. Can you see a way you may become fruitful in life now?

3. Is there anyone coming to mind you must release to free you to move forward?

4. Do you need to forgive yourself?

5. Have you ever stopped to listen to what your mind is saying?

6. What is the purpose you envision for yourself? For your family? For your business? For Your community? For the nation?

7. Is a closing ceremony a good consideration at this time? What would that be like for you?

8. What would total liberty look like for you?

Endnotes

1. Genesis 37:3, NKJV.
2. Genesis 37:2, NKJV.
3. Genesis 37:5-11, NKJV.
4. See Genesis 37:12-36, NKJV.
5. Genesis 39:1-9, NKJV.
6. See Genesis 39: 7-20, NKJV.
7. Genesis 39:23, NKJV.
8. See Genesis 40, NKJV.

9. Genesis 40:1-13, NKJV.

10. Genesis 41:26-40, NKJV.

11. Genesis 41:51, NKJV.

12. Ibid.

13. Genesis 41:52, NKJV.

14. II Corinthians 6:2, NKJV.

15. Genesis 45:5, NKJV.

16. Stump, Scott, *Parents Who Forgave Their Daughter's Killer, "It Frees Us,"* January 7, 2013 Accessed 14 October 2013, http://www.today.com/news/parents-who-forgave-their-daughters-killer-it-frees-us-1B7860708.

17. Ibid.

18. Ibid.

19. Ibid.

20. Concept learned through Restoring the Foundations (RTF) Ministries, http://rtfi.org

21. Frankl, Viktor, *Man's Search for Meaning,* (Boston Massachusetts: Beacon Press, 1959).

22. Genesis 37:1-13, NKJV.

23. Otis, Jr., George, *Transformations,* 1999.

24. Deuteronomy 30:19, NKJV.

YOU WILL FIND THAT
IT IS NECESSARY
TO LET THINGS GO;
SIMPLY FOR THE
REASON THAT THEY
ARE HEAVY. SO LET
THEM GO.

—C. JOYBELL C.

CHAPTER 9

THE SLEEPER MUST AWAKEN![1]

Rest is something we all need. However, if we are the ones pulling shift on guard duty, that is not the time to be sleeping! How would you feel if your life was left in someone else's hands, but he or she was just going to relax and not care what happened? You would not be able to rest if you knew your life was at stake. We realize there is a time to be awakened to what is really going on around us. The best news is God is at work in us and around us. We can be restored to our true spiritual and rightful place, but we must rise out of bed and prepare for an adventure. Just as some people are not morning people, some need extra measures or incentives to wake up. The same can be true for people who have experienced great loss to wake up to the reality and life before them.

DUNE SAID SO

One of my favorite movies is the 1984 version of *Dune*.[2] Frank Herbert's story was the catalyst to get me interested in reading. In a way, the book takes the Gospel and places it in a science fiction context. David Lynch captures the character and fortitude it takes to overcome the odds and loss in our lives. The father, Duke Leto Atreides, tells his son (Paul in the movie), "Something sleeps inside of us and seldom awakens. The sleeper must awaken!"[3] What had not yet awakened in Paul was how special he really was, nor did many realize how gifted he was. He was a type of Messiah that some had been breeding for, while others had been hoping for. Paul's father and his army, along with some of his best friends got slaughtered, but Paul did not get stuck in the loss. He awakened to what he could become. When the "Messiah" knew who he was and knew he could complete his mission, he inspired and mobilized the greatest fighting force the universe has ever seen, the Fremen. He brought these desert warriors out of darkness and into the light.[4]

This was science fiction, but our life is not! We are called to live each day to the fullest and pursue destiny. When we live to our fullest potential, like Paul Atreides, we also release others to achieve even greater works. Many times, in our American mindset, we think on an individual level. We only contemplate the impact of our actions on our personal lives. But around much of the world, many people groups have that "Fremen" mentality. They consider the consequences of their actions on the tribe, community, city, or nation. So let us consider this "Fremen" mentality and awaken to our destiny, with the understanding our personal revival will lead to communities, even generations getting on the fast track to a brighter future. Let us do everything we can to awaken now.

STOP HITTING THE SNOOZE BUTTON!

Do you know what it's like to live with a snoozer? A snoozer is someone who sets the alarm, but does not get up immediately after the alarm. He just repeatedly hits that snooze button, sometimes until it is too late. How do you break someone of this habit? You have to change the environment. One way to break the insanity is to place the alarm clock on the other side of the room rather than next to the bed. That way, the snoozer must actually arise in order to shut it off.

As the non-snoozer, the greatest struggle is to stop enabling the snoozer! If you are married, you know what I am talking about. If you come from a big family, you also know what I am talking about. Let me explain the life of a non-snoozer. We will make life easier for the snoozer because it just irritates us to hear the snooze alarm go off for the fourth time, especially when we are the ones who are already awake and have no trouble staying awake. We will help by bringing coffee, fixing their breakfast, warming up the car, etc. I know some of us do this out of love, specifically when our loved one appreciates acts of service. However, I am speaking about enabling behavior detrimental to the person.

Enabling can come in many different forms such as money, comfort, no responsibility, or a *carte blanche* full of excuses. Let us use one example, money. After a major loss, many people lose their focus on working. This can be understandable. In the case of a sudden, tragic death, the bereaved files paperwork and sorts the things left behind for months, sometimes lasting over a year. My dad was the executor of his brother's will and he spent eighteen months of his own time contacting banks, utilities, and friends along with sorting through his eighty years' worth of possessions. My dad was already retired, but it still took up the bulk of his time. We may start giving the bereaved person money so they can be taken care of, which is alright for a season. But a boundary should be set in place so that he knows when the wake-up call is coming. The best thing we can do for a loved one is get them back on the path of life after being stuck for a while. This process can be like a baby learning to walk. He will fall a few times before he gets the hang of it.

TURN THE LIGHTS ON!

My brother, Brian, is very creative. Back in our school days, he devised a way to assist in his morning routine to ensure he would awaken. Before the days of automatic light switches, Brian taped a string to the light switch, ran the string through some eye screws in the ceiling, then had the string hanging about three feet above his head. Once he pulled the string after the alarm, he had to wake up. Since there was no automatic way to shut the light back off, he had no choice but to get out of bed.

When it comes to spiritually awakening, illumination signifies placing the light on the subject. Searching for the truth is our way of turning the light on. The power of truth can never be underestimated because the truth is what can set people free.[5] Another key for us is to love the truth so we can be saved, healed or delivered.[6] For illumination to happen, we must ask some tough questions. And if we cannot ask the tough questions, then we must seek some trustworthy help and have someone else ask them. However, we are still on the hook for the answers.

As I have noted earlier, the whole truth being revealed does break us out of the cycle of grief and into the acceptance stage. Reviewing situations I had mentioned earlier from personal experience to a national crisis, let us be armed with some questions and answers that propel us forward in life. If your child lived through the Columbine shooting, did the event change the child's life? Yes. For the community what has happened? School is still a necessity because we value education. For the child, family and community, all may value life on a much greater scale and see a purpose much greater than anyone previously conceived. If a loved one was lost, the family's destiny has not changed, but how they live it out and who they live it out with has changed.

With the outcome of the elections in 2000, and 2012, did the outcome change our citizenship? Pleased or chagrined, we still stand behind our nation because we have a love for our country and our fellow countrymen. What are we willing to do to ensure unity within the nation? We have the capability to ensure a legitimate election by a receipt verifying who voted and who we voted for. If Iraq could do it, so can we!

The Black Boxes from the planes on 9/11 would bring a lot of illumination. Numerous questions could be answered and give many people a sense of peace and closure allowing for acceptance. But if our loved ones were on the plane or in the buildings and perished, their lives are not going to be brought back, no matter what facts are discovered. Their lives ended and for the people who remained what changed for them is the people they spend their lives with, the work place experience, the way we conduct business and travel and think about the world. Did our lives stop? No, but our lifestyle changed and our values shifted. For those of us in the military, we have left the comforts of home over and over again. We keep being sent back to a different culture—and an unusually hot climate most of the year—to carry out the orders of the elected and appointed officials dictating policy. Nationally we have traded security for freedom. Are we willing to swap back? Are we willing to embrace life to the fullest again? What would that look like for us?

STAY ALERT, STAY ALIVE!

The United States Military has the highest leadership training in the world. Other nations send their best qualified people to our schools. We do the same thing within our military, only allowing the very best enlisted personnel and officers to attend the classes, many of them being an accredited Master's degree. At the lower levels of the professional military education, most people are able to attend this in residence. When I was becoming a non-commissioned officer (NCO), I attended the Primary Leadership and Development Course (PLDC). One of our instructors repeatedly stated, "Stay alert, stay alive!"

Besides being pithy, essential meaning and deliberation is packed in this.

The goal is not just to be awake, but also be alert. In the physical, this can refer to our surroundings so we know what is around us as well as what is coming toward us or what we are moving toward. In our lives, we must be alert to the opportunities placed before us. Due to grief, numerous people missed opportunities directly in front of them and did not embrace them. Self-awareness becomes a key once again. We can be thankful God gives a second chance.[7] If we know we are distracted, this is where a trustworthy friend, colleague or therapist can be priceless. Staying alive does not just mean "staying alive," but living every day to our fullest potential. What are the essentials to creating a great day every day?

> STAYING ALIVE DOES NOT JUST MEAN "STAYING ALIVE," BUT LIVING

Corporate awareness is not just a dream, it is an achievable reality. I have witnessed military units possess such awareness of each other that the group could identify who was feeling down or sick without being in close proximity. A level of trust is established that continues to save lives. As an example, I have heard several stories of a unit member having a gut feeling not to take a certain route, voice it to the command, and hear the news of an ambush or improvised explosive device (IED) being exposed.

I know of a real estate development firm started by three men. These three men can look at a property, imagine the development, and calculate the cost in their heads and know within two hours if the business venture will work or not.

GETTING OUTSIDE ASSISTANCE

We can also gain awareness by someone else giving us the extra insight, motivation, or direction we need. In order for my dad to get out of bed for school, my grandma would flip his covers off and start snapping a wet towel! This may be considered unorthodox today, but my grandma knew what it took to get her boy out of bed!

When it comes to outside assistance, have you ever had someone proverbially hit you right between the eyes with what you truly needed to hear? To this day, you can probably still remember exactly what they said. I have had several "wake-up" calls in my life and I pray the same thing will arouse you out of slumber. Sometimes the warm blankets have grown a little too cozy and we really need an extra push out of bed.

Someone else's gifts can make a huge difference. These may be natural gifts, such as great listening skills or the ability to see concepts within the details of your life. Other gifts can be spiritual, such as discernment, wisdom, or faith.[8] We can have someone who knows us well give us the encouragement and direction we need to wake up and get out of the rut we have been stuck in.

Someone else's view can make a big difference precisely because it is not the same as ours! I love math, but sometimes I could not see how to solve a problem and get the answer.

My study partner could look at the same problem and have it solved in two steps. This can be true within our lives as well. Mentors, coaches, chaplains, counselors, doctors, ministers or rabbis have a different perspective than our own and usually have more experience or more training to give the proper directives.

Someone else's tools can get us out of the mud and back on the road again. Some tasks become amazingly simple when the right tool is available and used. Have you tried to pull a nail out with a screwdriver? What will you try if you do not have a hammer? When it comes to tools, this can also refer to resources like this book, a teaching, seminar, or counseling session. I have given some trustworthy resources as a separate appendix for your convenience.

WALK CIRCUMSPECTLY

We must walk circumspectly, which means vigilant or guarded. We must walk in wisdom and understanding in order to redeem the time, as William Wilberforce did in the British Empire in the 1800's. This one man had the goal to abolish slavery as well as make morality the cultural thing to do. He spent his lifetime pursuing these goals and saw them achieved, if only a few days before he died. Was it worth it for him? Absolutely! Was it worth it for the rest of the world? I hope you would say yes. He succeeded and so can we. History does have a way of repeating itself and we are facing similar issues in our time. We can become completely oblivious to what is happening around us if we are not careful.

We do not want to be complacent, but vigilant in prayer, guarded with our family, and watchful in the sphere where God has placed us. Would you want someone who is on guard duty to be napping when he is supposed to be protecting his sector? We should not be sleeping on the job either. But many of us have fallen asleep on the life we have been entrusted with. Our goal is to "make a profit" with our life so that a legacy is left behind that inspires others to exceed their potential, not just for us to reach ours.

RESTORING OUR VISION AND REMEMBERING OUR DREAMS

Have you ever awakened and remembered an extremely vivid dream? You remembered the scenes, the characters, and the imagery, along with the distinct feeling there was a purpose behind such a dream? Once we have awakened, we must not only remember our dreams, we must restore our vision. "Where there is no revelation, the people cast off restraint."[11] The revelation being discussed here is the kind that comes as prophetic vision or something we dream about. Many times, we have received dreams or visions like a seed planted in us. These seeds are meant to produce a life within us along with a purpose.

We may also have other dreams in the form of a passion or pursuit, as Viktor Frankl did when he envisioned himself teaching at the University in Austria once he obtained freedom from the Nazi death camps.[12] When we dream of our purpose or envision our calling, we can literally make it become a reality in our life. Sometimes, we may even have to give up something we are great at in order to pursue these dreams. Let me give you a few examples.

John Paul Jackson was a successful businessman making well over six figures by the age of thirty. However, through some divine intervention, he realized the business he was in was not his passion or his calling. He made that shift and pursued his dreams. John Paul Jackson actually has become a noted authority on dreams and dream interpretation.[13] When he interpreted dreams, he could do so with incredible accuracy, like a modern day Joseph. An older gentleman asked how he did this and Mr. Jackson responded he simply "did it," that was it. This wise gentleman responded, "That is too bad; your gift will die with you." The man's words cut to the heart and launched John Paul into his current business, which is his ministry of imparting his knowledge to assist people in understanding dreams and pursuing them.

Dr. Lance Wallnau has a similar story, being successful in business by the age of 25. He felt called to go into ministry and did so for several years as a pastor. However, something inside him realized something was missing, and not just for him. Lance kept meeting people who could not launch out into their life with their dreams and see them manifest as reality. So he dropped everything, moved his entire family to Dallas, and pursued the business of getting people to understand the mountain of influence they are called to and directing them with practical steps to pursue their vision and become masters in their sphere.[14]

A third example I would like to use is Rick Springfield. Yes, I enjoy his music and he put on one of the best concerts I saw in my life. But before he pursued music, he was actually a successful soap opera star. So why did he leave such a great career? The dream within Rick to be a musician was awakened, but had been dormant since he was a child. If you listen to his music, you know he lived through grief and loss. The passion of his heart was pursued like a cheetah going for a gazelle. He obtained what he dreamed.

So what is holding us back? This may not just be a personal question, but a familial, corporate, community or national one. When we awaken to who we are and where we are, we have the insight to get past our loss and see we have so much more to live for. Now is the time for the sleeper to awaken and get on the path of life and cross the threshold of destiny.

QUESTIONS TO CONSIDER

1. Are you awakened to your life and the potential you have?

2. Are we willing to embrace life to the fullest again? What would that look like for us?

3. What are the essentials to creating a great day every day?

4. Have you ever had someone proverbially hit you right between the eyes with what you truly needed to hear? What did they say?

5. Have you ever awakened and remembered an extremely vivid dream? What do you think it meant?

6. What is holding you back from your dreams?

Endnotes

1. *Dune*, Universal Pictures, 1984.

2. Ibid.

3. Ibid.

4. Herbert, Frank, *Dune*, 1965. (Radnor, PA: Chilton Book Company, 1965, 1984).

5. John 8:32, NKJV.

6. II Thessalonians 2:10, paraphrase mine.

7. Isaiah 11:11, AMP.

8. I Corinthians 12:7-12, NKJV.

9. *Taken*, 2009.

10. See www.love146.org or www.notforsalecampaign.org to learn more.

11. Proverbs 29:18a.

12. Frankl, Viktor, *Man's Search for Meaning*, (Boston, MA: Beacon Press, 2006).

13. Jackson, John Paul. "Understanding Dreams and Visions" Audio CD, (Flower Mound, TX: Streams Ministries International, 2003).

14. Wallnau, Lance, www.lancewallnau.com heard in person October 12, 2012.

DREAMS AND VISIONS
ARE LIKE SEEDS
PLANTED INSIDE US.
THEY ARE MEANT
TO GERMINATE
WITH PURPOSE
AND PRODUCE LIFE
WITHIN US.

CHAPTER 10

THE BREAKING OF A NEW DAWN

Now is the time for the dawning of a new day. Do not wait for another, make it today. A picture can be worth a thousand words, or more, in many cases. Below is my personal photo of when we changed the flag out at "Hero's Highway" at Joint Base Balad, Iraq, on October 1, 2010. We changed out the flag, which covered the entire ceiling of that tent, because a new mission began.

But what did the old flag represent? Hero's Highway was the covering from the helipad to the emergency room at the hospital. Hero's Highway was placed there to give wounded service members shelter from the sun or from the rain, depending on the season. Sometimes, the Balad Hospital would be so busy wounded personnel would need to be triaged outside and wait in Hero's Highway for space to open up. Every wounded or dying soldier, sailor, airman or marine who came via helicopter passed under that old flag.

I do not know how many of those young men and women passed under that flag, but many of them remember seeing the big stars and stripes above them. On one side of that flag, all that was lost was somewhere out there, in the past. After passing under that flag, everything that could be done to save a life would be accomplished by some of the most skilled people I have ever witnessed. The future waited on the other side of the flag, whatever that would look like for the wounded hero. Many of them lost friends and comrades in arms who were not even given a chance to pass under the flag, because they had already departed this life. Many of the survivors lost limbs, or eyesight, or more, but life was still to be lived on the other side of Hero's Highway. No matter what life looked like, they were still willing to embrace it and move forward.

When a new mission began, the flag was properly retired in a ceremony. A new flag kicked off the new mission, Operation New Dawn. The new flag was not representative of all the loss. The drawdown officially commenced and our forces would be out of Iraq the following calendar year, giving two countries an opportunity for a new beginning. Is it time for a flag change and a new mission in your life?

A NEW PASSIONATE DESTINATION

What would a new beginning look like for you? Since we have made it to this point, we had to deal with the loss and have the courage to go ahead in our lives. We must fold up the memories of what was and focus on what is to come. For many of us, this can be defined as our second chance in life. Even if we start off with a rocky beginning, showing initiative to get back at the helm of our own lives will speak volumes to our friends and loved ones around us. Our actions will also be our own witness. We must have a new passion in life and discover what our purpose is following a loss. This can be half the battle.

Passion may give us the energy and motivation, but we must also have a destination in mind. Even with a full tank of gas, we do not want to go four hundred miles in the wrong direction and end up in another cycle of grief. We must remove all doubt and dare to dream big. We should dream of the impossible happening!

For instance, what if you had an interest in painting a work of art, but had never attempted it? What if you decided to pick it up as a hobby? What would happen if others enjoyed or were moved by your work? What would happen if your works of art started selling big? What if your way of making a living also became your passion? How would that change your life? How would that change the lives of your children and grandchildren? How would your community or city be affected by your success?

A DIFFERENT RESPONSE

An event plus our response gives us the outcome.[1] Generating a different response after a tremendous or traumatic loss can seem impossible. But with God, nothing is impossible.[2] I believe God likes it when we pray for the impossible to happen. I believe God likes it even more when we make the impossible happen through our own actions or events, whether personally or corporately. Whatever it takes, we must generate a different response in order to come to that place of acceptance.

Do you think it is possible God is working in the midst of the disasters and our trauma to elicit a different response out of us? Let me explain what I mean. New Orleans was devastated in 2005. It just so happens, in the fifth year following the impact of Katrina and Rita, the New Orleans Saints won the Superbowl. In a city where mourning had almost become a profession, the people were given a reason to celebrate. They were actually given an occasion to cause a different response. Many ministers caught on to that and held their respective memorial services to bring closure and enable the city to move forward.

Now there is the case for Boston. The Boston Marathon bombing is still a complete shock to many of us. This not only bewildered the city, but baffled the nation. Yet the Boston Red Sox won the World Series shortly after on October 30, 2013. A city covered in mourning overflowed with effusive festivities filled with joy. The citizens of Boston have something to replace the trauma throughout the rest of its existence.

When it came to our nation, after September 11, 2001, which team won the Superbowl? The New England "Patriots" won their *first* Superbowl ... and they happened to be from the "American" Football Conference. Is this too much to be a mere coincidence? Could we take this as a sign there is a victory in store for American patriots? If this can happen on a national scale, what is happening to us on a personal level? Do we notice the little details within our sphere? We are told "those who sow in tears shall reap in joy."[3] The joy is just one response meant to take us out of the ditch and get us back on the path of life. We must be attentive every day for the opportunities we have to pursue a greater outcome on every facet of our life.

LAUGH AT THE DAYS TO COME

Nothing changes our mood, outlook or circumstances like humor. Gallows humor is prominent within the military, especially in places where trauma is a part of normal life. I have noticed this kind of humor on the civilian side as well. When I covered the "on call" duties in the Emergency Room of a Level I Trauma Center, I was shocked at first by the things I heard. As I gained more experience, I realized this phenomenon must have been designed in us to reframe traumatic events with a different response.

Laughter can literally induce healing in our bodies, but I believe it goes beyond our bodies and into our souls. Solomon, the wisest man who lived, wrote, "A merry heart does good, like medicine."[4]

When it comes to laughing, one couple did not have much of a reason to laugh. Over 5700 years ago, Abraham was told he would become the father of many nations. He was also told he would have a child of promise through his wife, Sarah. This all sounds great, but Sarah had an issue. She was barren in a culture and time when having children was a sign of God's blessing. Yet, she went past the age to have children naturally.

Even though Sarah was told she would produce an heir to her husband, Abraham, the deferred hope of this happening made her heart sick.[5] Then three strangers showed up at Abraham's and Sarah's dwelling one day, and Abraham offered them hospitality. One of the foreigners asked where she was and Abraham replied she was in the tent. One of the men said Sarah would have a son by the time he returned in the next year. Sarah laughed within herself because she was well past the age of childbearing.[6] Now the questions I have following this encounter cannot really be answered with our knowledge. Was Sarah healed in her soul and body by God, by the laughter, or both? If laughter impacts the body and soul, I would like to know.

We may not know the answer, but we do know the outcome. Sarah did indeed conceive, many believe at the age of 90, and gave birth to a son. Now the funny part is Abraham named the boy Isaac, which means "He laughs!"[7] So every time Abraham and Sarah called his name, they were reminded of laughter. Perhaps God has a greater sense of humor than we ever give Him credit for! But do you see what this name did? Every time Abraham and Sarah heard the name, they were declaring laughter. All the years of their deferred hope ended in laughter, were filled with laughter, and were reminded of laughter. So what would need to happen for us to carry laughter in our lives? We must do whatever it takes to bring laughter in our lives. A daily dose of laughter should be a prescription for us to be healthy.

DO WE HAVE THE HEZEKIAH COMPLEX?

As we move forward, we must continue to evaluate our motives as well as our actions. What if we used our business prowess to create a huge fortune, but wasted it on ourselves? What would be the benefit for future generations? What if we created a family trust or foundation with the amassed wealth creating a stream of revenue that keeps giving in perpetuity? The truth is many people who have survived trauma or loss actually did become successful. The "Nifty Fifties" happened because a large number of war veterans went into business and were very successful at it. Did they consider where the future generations would take their success? Did they consider some would take it for granted? Is it possible for us to overlook outcomes because of the peace and prosperity in our days?

We do not want to be the people who mortgage the future because of our own personal attitude or decisions. We must do everything possible to avoid the mistake Hezekiah made toward the end of his life. We must pursue the future as our own and leave a legacy that is worthwhile for the generations ahead. Rather than thinking of us, we can learn from one great example, who had the cure for the Hezekiah Complex before it was diagnosed. Let us consider what our imagination was given for and how we can use it to influence a prosperous future instead of an indentured one.

THE CURE IS IMAGINATION!

What will your actions cause? What will be the effects of our choices fifty years from now? General Omar Bradley defined imagination as the "the quality that enables him to anticipate the train of consequences that would follow from his contemplated courses of action."[8] A world champion chess player can picture the whole board and imagine what the next nine moves will look like. How many of us think in terms like this? In the United States, most people do not think six months ahead. As a good example, most of us think in two week blocks. Based on the example of the average pay check cycle, we have our bills and expenses figured out for two weeks so the bills can be paid and we can hit the reset button for the next two weeks. If we thought six months ahead, we would have six months of income in the bank and not be concerned about the pay check two weeks from now.

When it comes to a personal vision or goal, do we have something set for even one year from now? Do we have one for five years? Ten years? What are your goals for your family or community? Have you imagined what your city will look like in fifty years? What if Detroit would have done this kind of imagination fifty years ago? Did you know Los Angeles had one of the greatest electronic trolley systems in the world in 1936? What if the city would have imagined the issues with traffic and smog due to exponential growth? Did you know some Japanese corporations have a three hundred year plan? What did the Japanese learn Lehman Brothers did not? As a leader in your community, what future do you perceive? As a business owner, what are you imagining in this moment?

BEING FRUITFUL LIKE AN APPLE

I have appreciated Apple® as a company since I bought an Apple® IIGS in 1989. I was so impressed with the "1 meg" of memory it came with! Many people wondered if this company would go on and survive with all the competition out there since it ran on a different operating system than IBM®. In the mid to late 1990's, the company seemed to be on the very edge of survival, maybe just hanging on by life support. But something happened. What was it? Books, business journals, biographies, documentaries, and movies want to answer this burning question. The truth is there may be more than one answer.

Apple® became the #1 brand name in 2013, surpassing Google® and Coca Cola®.⁹ What if Apple® had stopped looking forward in 2008? What if Steve Jobs and their executives had been content and stopped there? We could have picked a date when they were not as successful, but the company kept a core value I will label as fruitfulness. I would say this is across the company spectrum from how Apple® treats their customers, their employees, their quality, their creativity, and their engineering.

Whether at the top or the bottom, we cannot settle and become stagnant. Perception can be reality, but we cannot fake fruitfulness. The only reason a body of water becomes toxic for life is when there ceases to be an outflow. So long as a stream or river continues to feed it and the water continues to have a way out, life happens. Interestingly, one of the most productive bodies of water is the Sea of Galilee with the Jordan River being the main water flowing in and out of the lake. However, the Jordan River continues into the Dead Sea, which has no outlet and no life. The fruitfulness is dependent upon the outflow. If we want to be bountiful, let us consider how fruitful we are being in our own lives as well as in the lives of the people around us.

WE CANNOT FAKE FRUITFULNESS

How can we be more fruitful in our own lives? Have we considered our family or friends? How can we influence our community or city? As a business owner, how would a culture of fruitfulness change the way you or your business is perceived? As a nation, what would we define as fruitful? On a national level, this is truly a multi-trillion dollar question.

REACHING THE SUMMIT

If we were given the opportunity to climb Mount Everest, would we have a goal of reaching the base camp or reaching the summit? We would go for the summit, of course! This may seem silly, but many of us have done this in our lives, especially after a major loss. We figure if we aim a little lower, we will not be as disappointed the next time. We must demolish this kind of thinking and have the overcomer's attitude of shooting for the moon.

As an example, let us look at the oncology world. The summit would be a total cure for cancer. The base camp would be a momentary response. One of my heroes, Dr. Edward B. Arenson, Jr. (Dr. A), is leading the fight in treating and curing primary malignant brain tumors. He has an overcoming attitude when it comes to curing Glioblastoma Multiforme (GBM), which is synonymous with a WHO Grade IV[10] primary brain tumor. In many circles, a GBM is considered a death sentence and most people only give the standard of care. The "standard of care" is what the FDA recommends and what the health insurance companies will pay for. The goal of the "standard of care" is to achieve a response for the best possible outcome, but its goal is not cure. If the goal were cure in the realm of oncology, then doctors would be allowed to practice medicine.

The oncology world was actually revolutionized thanks to Tuberculosis. Tuberculosis (TB) was treated the way some cancer is treated now. One antibiotic would be given and cause a positive response for a while, but the TB would come back and eventually kill the patient. However, one doctor thought outside the box and gave three strong antibiotics simultaneously, resulting in TB being cured. Now TB has been practically wiped out in North America. Many forms of cancer have now been cured due to this same philosophy. Doctors started administering three or more different forms of chemotherapy at once and the results speak for themselves. Some forms of cancer are now considered a setback like the cold or flu, but used to be completely fatal.

When it comes to curing GBM, Dr. A. has been tenacious. He has fought with health insurance companies, medical boards, neurosurgeons, and anyone else who would stand in the way of him treating his patients. Many times he would skip his doctor fee so a patient could afford the treatment the health insurance company refused. He uses the philosophy of combining three or more chemotherapy treatments at once. What were the results? He had 122 patients invited to the Long Term Survivors Party in 2013. A patient cannot be invited unless he is three years out or more from the time of diagnosis. These patients and their families are very grateful they have a doctor who aims for the summit called cure.

What would our goal be in our respective calling, career or business? Would we aim to be the best or would we settle for mediocre? What would happen to your favorite team if the coach had a goal of winning three games this year rather than taking the championship? That coach would be fired today and replaced immediately with someone who can imagine the best possible outcome. The same is true for a business leader, pastor, rabbi, politician, teacher, doctor or any other field we are a part of. So where does this leave us? If we will not follow someone with a mediocre measure, then we cannot settle for a mediocre mindset in our own life. Even if the odds are against us, the sweat and sacrifice is worth it for the sake of our lineage, not just us.

FROM FLOUNDERING
TO FLOURISHING

Can we approach life with a sense of positive expectation? None of us know when our time of deliverance or breakthrough will occur. If we aim for nothing, that is exactly what we will get. If we do not live every day to the fullest and nurture our future, then we have already settled. The last thing we want to have happen is to slip back into the ditch after we have managed to get back on the road!

In order for a new dawn to take place, we must go back to the beginning of where we started this journey and think of it like driving. We do not want to be stuck in the mud again. Once we have our speed up and our gaze fixed on the horizon, our momentum will propel us forward. If we keep looking into our rear view mirror, we will lose sight of where we are going and veer off the road. Our lives are like that if we dwell on the past too much without looking ahead. If we are distracted, we take our foot off the accelerator and slow down. We actually start to flounder instead of moving forward.

We may miss the scenic route filled with all kinds of opportunities. The scenic route can be filled with all kinds of adventures we were not anticipating. Have you ever had a beautiful memory created because of an opportunity you experienced?

When it comes to flourishing, I want you to picture yourself like an oak tree planted near the bank of a river. You bring forth fruit in your season, and your leaves are always green in.[11] No matter what the circumstances are, you will flourish because you have the basics to be continually fruitful. If life throws a drought, storm, harsh winter or flood your way, you will be able to stand because your roots are firmly planted and your foundation cannot be shaken. Even if some kind of treatment were needed, you need to remember you are not alone. God is for you. I am for you. You have a community you belong to. If you are not involved or plugged in, find a safe and healthy group you connect with.

NO MATTER YOUR CIRCUMSTANCES, YOU WILL FLOURISH BECAUSE YOU HAVE THE BASICS TO BE CONTINUALLY FRUITFUL

Thank you for allowing me to accompany you on this journey. My hope is you were able to identify the points in your life where you might feel "stuck." As life continues, I hope you feel equipped to tackle grief and loss head on so you can come to a place of acceptance as quickly as possible in the future. I hope you feel empowered to identify the ditches you were in as well as those of your family, community, business, city, region and nation so that you can be a catalyst for change. My prayer for you is to "prosper and be in health just as your soul prospers."[12]

POINTS TO PONDER

1. Is it time for a flag change and a new mission in your life?

2. What would a new beginning look like for you?

3. What if our way of making a living also became our passion?

4. Do you think it is possible God is working in the midst of the disasters and our trauma to elicit a different response out of us?

5. What will your actions cause? What will be the effects of your choices fifty years from now?

6. What are you imagining in this moment? Where does your imagination take you fifty years from now?

7. How would a culture of fruitfulness change the way you or your business is perceived?

8. Is your goal to hit the base camp or the summit?

9. What is the difference between floundering and flourishing for you?

Endnotes

1. Canfield, Jack, *The Success Principles: How to Get from Where You Are to Where You Want to Be.* (New York, NY: HarperCollins Publishers, 2005).

2. Luke 1:37, NKJV.

3. Psalm 126:5, NKJV.

4. Proverbs 17:22, NKJV.

5. Proverbs 13:12, NKJV.

6. See Genesis 18:1-12, NKJV.

7. Genesis 21:3, NKJV.

8. Bradley, Omar, "On Leadership," from *Parameters XI,* no. 3 (September 1981): 2-7.

9. Rudderham, Tom, *Tech Conquers the World as Apple becomes number 1 Most Valued Brand,* accessed September 30, 2013 http://iosguides.net/apple-number-1-valued-brand/.

10. World Health Organization categories for tumors, IV being the most aggressive.

11. Psalm 1:3.

12. 3 John 2.

CHAPLAIN
WADE A. JENSEN

Chaplain Wade A. Jensen is assigned as the Wing Chaplain to the 153d Airlift Wing (AMC), Cheyenne ANG Base, WY. His responsibilities include the administering of religious rites; augmenting the Chapel's Contemporary Worship Experience; and providing unit visitation and counseling to the 153d Airlift Wing along with the other Joint Service Components and their dependents which are present in Wyoming.

Prior to entering the Air Force, Jensen served in the U.S. Army as a French Cryptologic Linguist from 1987-1991. He was mobilized in Desert Shield/Desert Storm during this time. He served at churches in Wyoming and South Dakota from 1995 to 2001.

He was the Chaplain and Patient Care Coordinator for the Colorado Neurological Institute (CNI) from 2006 to 2011. Chaplain Jensen deployed to Joint Base Balad, Iraq, where he served as the hospital chaplain from July 2010 to January 2011.

Upon his return, he continued to Serve CNI as a Chaplain and then as a Development Officer from June 2011 to August 2012.

Wade is passionate to help men and women escape the cycle of grief and move into a fulfilled and purposeful life. He is a patriot and deeply desires for America to awaken and resume her role as the pursuer of dreams and champion of liberty around the globe. He is married to Heather and together they have three children—Emily, Tiffany, and Noah. They reside in Cheyenne, Wyoming.

APPENDIX

ASSISTING AGENCIES, MINISTRIES AND PEOPLE

- **Jack Canfield:** *The Success Principles: How to Get from Where You Are to Where You Want to Be.* (New York, NY: HarperCollins Publishers, 2005).
  www.jackcanfield.com

- **Cleansing Stream Ministries:** they have a reputation for helping people with a proven track record going back decades.
  www.cleansingstream.org

- **Discovery!** Austin is a safe venue where you can go and be genuine about your life and receive healing, comfort, and purpose.
  www.discovery-austin.org

- **Doug Addison:** life coach, dream interpreter and comedian! Having overcome so much, he has a uniqueness to assisting others.
  www.dougaddison.com

- **Heather Jensen and Empowered to Rise:** certified Life Coach, relentless optimist, professional speaker, and my wife! She has a unique gift for assisting others.
  www.empoweredtorise.com

- **John Paul Jackson and Streams Ministries International:** they will assist you in dreaming again and interpreting your dreams. *www.streamsministries.com*

- **Lance Wallnau and the Lance Learning Group:** Lance has a gift for helping people overcome their past hurts and failures and encourages them to launch out into their life purpose on the Seven Mountains of Culture. *www.lancewallnau.com*

- **Marked Men for Christ and Women Walking with Christ:** they provide a safe space with a group of like-minded people who want to be genuine and free. *www.markedmenforchrist.org*

- **Pure Desire Ministries International:** Many people get caught up in sexual issues due to past grief, loss and trauma. Dr. Ted Roberts speaks with authority and experience of how to break free of these addictions. *www.puredesire.org*

- **Rabbi Daniel Lapin:** *www.rabbidaniellapin.com*

- **Restoring the Foundations (RTF), International:** They have a network of counselors across the United States and can work with individuals or couples. *www.rtfi.org*

- **Truth:** The truth has power in any form. Ultimately, from my experience, The Truth is a person named Jesus and He can assist in you getting completely free. *See John 8:32-36; 14:6*

BOOKS

- Addison, Doug, *Understand Your Dreams Now: Spiritual Dream Interpretation*, (Santa Maria, CA: InLight Connection, 2013).

- Andrews, Andy, *Storms of Perfection*, (Nashville, TN: Lightning Crown Publishers, 1991).

- Augustine of Hippo, *The City of God*, translated by Marcus Dods (Peabody, MA: Hendrickson Publishers, Inc., 2010).

- The Bible! This one book has all things pertaining to life and godliness. Pick a translation and pick a language, the best-selling book of all time!

- Bruce-Hamburger, Shauna, *Beyond Adversity into Freedom*, (Sevierville, TN: Insight Publishing Co., 2010). Find more at www.divinepotential.com.

- Frankl, Viktor, *Man's Search for Meaning*, (Boston Massachusetts: Beacon Press, 1959).

- Joyner, Rick, *I See a New America*, (Ft. Mill, SC: Quest Ventures, 2011).

- Kubler-Ross, Elizabeth, *On Death and Dying*, First Classic Scribner Edition (New York: Scribner, 1969, 1997).

- Kubler-Ross, Elisabeth and David Kessler, *On Grief and Grieving: Finding the Meaning of Grief through the Five Stages of Loss* (New York: Scribner, 2005).

- Kushner, Harold, *When Bad Things Happen to Good People* (New York, NY: AnchorBooks, a Division of Random House Publishing, 1981, 2004).

- Lewis, C.S., *A Grief Observed* (New York, NY: HarperCollins Publishers, 1961, 1989).

- Lewis, C.S., *The Problem of Pain* (New York, NY: HarperCollins Publishers, 1962, 1989).

- Morell, David, *The Successful Novelist*, (Naperville, IL: Sourcebooks, Inc., 2008).

- Seahorn, Janet J. and E. Anthony, *Tears of a Warrior: A Family's Story of Combat and Living*

- Sheets, Dutch, *Tell Your Heart to Beat Again*, (Ventura, CA: Gospel Light Publications, 2002).

- Walters, Wendy K., *Intentionality: Live on Purpose!*, (Keller, TX: Palm Tree Productions, 2012).

- Walters, Wendy K., *Marketing Your Mind* (Keller, TX: Palm Tree Productions, 2011).

- Westberg, Granger E., *Good Grief*, (Minneapolis, MN: Fortress Press, 1962, 1971, 1997, 2011).

HUMOR

Anything (hopefully decent) making you laugh to the point of crying is worth your healing and edification. Here are a few of my personal recommendations.

- **Doug Addison:** *www.dougaddison.com*

- **Taylor Mayson:** *www.taylormason.com*

- **Tim Hawkins:** *www.timhawkins.net*

- **Thor Ramsey:** *www.thorramsey.com*

MOVIES

- *The Bucket List* (2007) is a must see for anyone who has gone through grief and loss.

- *Tuesdays with Morrie* (1999) was a book made into a TV series that explores several viewpoints of what people may experience in their grief and loss.

- *Unstoppable* (2013) with Kirk Cameron is taking *When Bad Things Happen to Good People* and exploring your faith with a Christian perspective.